FINDING GOD IN

THE HUNGER GAMES

FINDING GOD IN

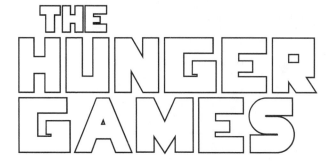

KEN GIRE

Published by eChristian, Inc.
Escondido, California

eChristianBooks

Finding God in The Hunger Games

Copyright © 2012 Ken Gire. All rights reserved.

First printing in 2012 by eChristian, Inc.
eChristian, Inc.
2235 Enterprise Street, Suite 140
Escondido, CA 92029
http://echristian.com

ISBN: 978-1-61843-259-9

Cover and interior design by Larry Taylor

Edited by Linda Washington

Produced with the assistance of Livingstone, the Publishing Services Division of eChristian, Inc. Project staff includes: Afton Rorvik, Linda Taylor, Ashley Taylor, Andy Culbertson, Joel Bartlett, Brittany Buczynski, Lois Jackson, and Tom Shumaker.

Printed in the United States of America

19 18 17 16 15 14 13 12 8 7 6 5 4 3 2 1

DEDICATED TO

The Katniss and Peeta that live in the hearts of
  Samantha
  Caleb
  Logan
  Ellaray
  Emery Lu
  and Fiona

CONTENTS

In the ruins of a place once known as North America . . .

From the back cover of *The Hunger Games* by Suzanne Collins

AUTHOR'S FOREWORD

I grew up in the idyllic world of the 1950s, where you could escape hot summer nights by slipping under the fence of the Westerner Drive-In, spreading out a blanket, and sitting in lawn chairs with a cooler of ice-cold lemonade and a grocery sack of hot, buttered popcorn.

To escape the swelter of a summer afternoon—"polio weather," as my mother called it—you could take in a matinee at the River Oaks Theater with its refrigerated air and its seduction of snacks.

Both that drive-in and that indoor theater have closed.

But the memories linger.

For as long as I can remember, film has played an important role in my life—from an adventure-seeking boy to a star-struck teenager to an adult craving a couple hours of escape from the scorching realities of life.

I believe that film is the most powerful medium in the history of storytelling. Larger-than-life images looming in our imaginations long after the curtain has come down and the lights have gone up. Living within us. To caution us, perhaps. Or to inspire us to throw all caution to the wind. Who knows how the images will lead us ... or mislead us.

Because of the importance of images in our society, I am drawing from the film of *The Hunger Games* rather than the book. I'm sure each of us had an image of what Katniss Everdeen looked like from her description in the book, but ever since Jennifer Lawrence stepped into the role, it's hard to imagine anyone but her playing the part.

The same with Peeta Mellark, played by Josh Hutcherson.

And could anyone have played Haymitch Abernathy better than Woody Harrelson?

Or President Snow better than Donald Sutherland?

Another reason for choosing the film is that I have ADD, and watching a film is easier for me than reading a book. In a book, I get distracted, think about other things, put it down, get a snack, pick it up again, put it down again, often not finishing it. With a movie, though, it's different. I sit still and stay still, totally focused.

Because of that, I have had more significant encounters with film than I have had with books. If you've read almost any of my books, you'll find film references everywhere. And when I speak, I seldom do so without a film clip to illustrate some point I'm trying to make.

I believe that writers, when they're really listening to their work, write more than they know. Certainly that was true of the biblical writers. Perhaps it is also true of the writer of *The Hunger Games*.

A lot has been written on the subject of God in Suzanne Collins's story. The purpose of this book is not to critique someone else's conclusions, let alone condemn them. It is not meant to spark debate but merely contribute to the discussion.

It is one person's opinion.

This is what that person saw in the dark, however dimly.

 **INTRODUCTION**

I wish the inspiration for my books came in predictable ways so it would make the process of deciding what to write next less ambiguous. But ambiguity, I have discovered, is part of the process. An important part. It is the part where certainty and uncertainty are separated by a chasm that only faith can bridge.

This book, for example.

I was reading *The Hunger Games* partly because my son and granddaughter had recommended it. And partly because it seemed the entire world was reading it.

Which intrigued me.

So I bought the book and started reading. After finishing a third of it, I began seeing posters for the movie everywhere, along with teasers on TV and trailers in theaters.

Which intrigued me even more.

During this time, the small group I attend took a week off from meeting and decided to go out to dinner instead. One of the people in the group e-mailed me the name of the restaurant: Bread and Circuses Bistro.

Odd name for a restaurant, I thought.

I googled directions, and it was in Towson, practically a suburb of

Baltimore. I had meant to ask the waiter what the significance of the name was, but I was distracted by the conversations of my friends and forgot.

A few days later another friend asked where we had eaten, and I said, "A place called Bread and Circuses. Weird name, huh? For a restaurant."

She told me that Suzanne Collins, author of the book, drew inspiration for her story from the Roman practice of controlling the citizens of the capital by providing them "bread and circuses"—free food and free entertainment.

Later I googled the website, which read:

> Bread and Circuses Bistro and Bar serves contemporary American cuisine with a bohemian flare. Come enjoy an authentic bistro dining experience in a cozy 1920s Towson haunt. We serve lunch, dinner, and lite fare; with a full bar, wine list, and coffee bar.

When you click "Events," it takes you to another page that tells you the nights when they have musical groups, ranging from Tapestry Eiran, which plays Celtic music, to OHO, "Baltimore's answer to Pink Floyd":

> Food and entertainment.
>
> Bread . . . and circuses.

I googled to see if there might be other restaurants by that name. There were two. One in Winnipeg; the other in Moscow. When I realized the one where I had eaten was the only one in the United States, it gave me pause. *What are the odds?* I thought.

That same week, my agent contacted me about writing a short book on *The Hunger Games.* I said yes, then went to see the film.

My understanding of the images in the film came slowly. What I want to do as a writer is to invite you, the reader, to walk with me through that process: to see how I arrived at my conclusions. And, along the way, to arrive at conclusions of your own.

I went to see the film a second time. This time I brought a notebook and pen. As my eyes adjusted to the dark, I watched and took notes. Afterward, I finished reading the book. I read blogs of people who either loved the film or hated it. I researched various film and social critics, some who found it entertaining, others who found it enlightening, and still others who found it revolting. I read interviews by the author, the cast, the director. I also watched them on video, talking about the story and what attracted them to it.

I prayerfully reflected on all of this.

Which led to what follows . . .

PART I

The Cinematic Story

You know this world, where it's easy to get confused between
reality and reality TV.

You know this place, where rich and poor live side by side
but worlds apart.

You, too, might question the choices a government makes
on your behalf.

You, too, have seen the environment abused, damaged beyond
repair.

This place is Panem, the world of *The Hunger Games*.

Kate Egan
The World of the Hunger Games

THE STORY

The Official Trailer
http://youtu.be/mfmrPu43DF8
2 minutes, 38 seconds

Opening weekend of *The Hunger Games,* the 2012 LionsGate film that was directed by Gary Ross, broke box-office records. Because of the crowds, I avoided opening weekend, opting instead for a weekday matinee. By now, I reasoned, the truants who had skipped school to see it were dutifully back at their desks, texting film reviews to their classmates.

When I arrived at the theater, it was plastered with posters. The cast was impressive, a mixture of familiar faces and fresh ones. Half of them I knew; the other half I didn't. Here are the ones I knew.

Jennifer Lawrence played Katniss Everdeen, the heroine. I had seen her in the small, independent film, *Winter's Bone,* for which she had been nominated for a Best Actress Oscar, and deservedly so.

Woody Harrelson, who played Haymitch Abernathy, Katniss and Peeta's mentor in the games, was noted for his comedic role as the naïve midwestern bartender in the sitcom, *Cheers,* as well as for his more serious roles in films such as *No Country for Old Men* (2007), in which he played a professional assassin.

Elizabeth Banks I had seen in the inspirational movie, *Invincible,* in which she played charmingly opposite Mark Wahlberg. In this film she played a cartoonish character who shuffled through her scenes in heels too high, clothes too tight, makeup too thick, hair too teased, and hats too outlandish even for the outlandish fashions in the Capitol.

Lenny Kravitz, the really cool, world-renowned singer, played the equally cool and supportive Cinna, Katniss and Peeta's fashion designer.

Stanley Tucci, who has starred and costarred in such films as *Big Night* (1996) and *Road to Perdition* (2002) played Caesar Flickerman, the blue-haired, big-smiled television host and the game's flamboyant announcer.

And, finally, the 76-year-old veteran, Donald Sutherland. He played the sly, snakish dictator, President Coriolanus Snow. I think I first saw him in *The Eye of the Needle* (1981), then years later in *Ordinary People* (1980), and *Backdraft* (1991).

I handed my ticket to a woman, who tore it and directed me to the "second theater on the left." I settled into a seat in the dark as the story flickered to life.

The film begins with a black screen and white lettering, setting the stage for the story by telling its backstory. In penance for their revolt, each district was to send two tributes between 12 and 18 years old that had been selected in a random drawing at a public gathering known as "The Reaping." These 24 tributes were to fight to the death until only one remained. This contest was known as The Hunger Games.

> From the treaty of the treason: In penance for their uprising,
>   each district shall offer up a male and female between the
>   ages of 12 and 18 at a public "Reaping."
> These Tributes shall be delivered to the custody of the Capitol.
>   And then transferred to a public arena where they will
>   fight to the death until a lone victor remains.
> Henceforth and forevermore this pageant shall be known as
>   The Hunger Games.

Cut to:

The first scene, showing the inside of a plain home, sparsely furnished. The 16-year-old Katniss cradling her 12-year-old sister, Prim, in her arms. Looking at her, tenderly. Then tucking her in bed. Singing to her, softly.

A maternal moment.

Which makes me wonder where their mother is.

Cut to:

Outside her home. The tumbledown neighborhood looking like a Depression-era photograph. Awash with the bleakest of colors. Shadowy blacks, weathered grays, hopeless blues. Clapboard houses with their paint peeled off. No yards. No fences. Nothing green or flowery. Just the worn-out earth. And the worn-out faces on slump-shouldered adults. Threadbare clothes on barefoot kids. Lean-looking, all of them.

Suddenly I know a lot about this unlikely heroine. The hardscrabble life she's lived. The make-do-or-do-without realities that have shaped her. You can see it in her neighborhood, her home, but mostly you can see it in her eyes, which look as if the life's been drained from them.

Cut to:

Katniss escaping the confines of her district by lifting an electrified, barb-wired fence, which she does confidently, as if she has figured out the times during the day when the Capitol shuts off the power.

Cut to:

The forest, where she retrieves her bow and arrows that she's kept hidden in the hollow of a tree. She pulls an arrow from the quiver and puts it on the string, drawing it back, ready to shoot anything that shows itself.

She moves stealthily.

Then . . .

A rustling of branches. She turns. A deer. She pulls her bowstring, waiting for her shot. The deer moves warily, in and out of the foliage. It stops behind a bush. She replaces the arrow with a rock. Shoots it in the deer's direction to flush it out.

Before she can take her shot, though, a male voice calls to her, spooking the deer. She lets her arrow fly, but the deer's a blur, its white tail up in the air as it bounds into the forest.

She whips around.

Cut to:

Gale. Tall, good-looking, strong. A winsome smile on his face.

She is irritated, but he kids her out of it.

Cut to:

Both of them padding through the woods. He throws a rock to flush a covey of what looks like quail. In a move as swift as it is sure, she zings an arrow into one of them, impaling her family's dinner.

The moment is interrupted by the threatening whir of an approaching hovercraft. They duck into the bushes. In a moment, it passes. They are safe, at least for now, but it feels like an ominous foreshadowing.

O)

I took notes like this—in the dark—for the entire movie. Page after page of them. Scribbling scenes and lines of dialogue as fast as I could. By the end of the film, I almost had to pry the pen from my fingers as I watched. I had written so fast I didn't have time to reflect on anything I saw. And by now I was hungry. Emerging from the cool cave of the theater into the glare of a midday sun, I squinted as my eyes tried to adjust. Then I saw it.

A burger place. Less than a block from the theater.

I had been to the circus; now it was time to go for the bread.

My thinking? To leaf through my notebook while eating, reflecting on the inspiration that had eluded me in the theater. Certainly my hunger had distracted me.

After two hours and 24 minutes without food, everything on the menu looked good.

Cheeseburger. The works. Fries. Fresh and hand-cut. These are my people. Mm? Shake or soft drink?

The cheeseburger, I reasoned, represented all the major food groups (meat, vegetables, grains), so I splurged. Got the soft drink and the shake.

I nested into a booth at the far end, not far from the soda machine. And I started to reflect . . .

Like most cinematic stories, *The Hunger Games* was told in a three-act structure, first popularized by Aristotle in his small treatise on drama, titled *Poetics*. In it, he proposed that dramatic action can be broken down into a beginning, a middle, and an end. As the protagonist encounters greater and greater obstacles, his or her character is made visible not so much through words but through action. During the course of the story, this character goes through a series of changes, emerging as a different person in the end, hopefully a better person.

First, I sketched the structure of the story.

The inciting incident that starts the story? Prim's name getting drawn from the fishbowl at the Reaping and Katniss volunteering to take her place.

Blake Snyder in his 2005 book, *Save the Cat!*, describes this as "the 'Save the Cat' scene. . . . It's the scene where we meet the hero and the hero does something—like saving a cat—that defines who he is and makes us, the audience, like him."

Immediately we like Katniss because she saves something so much more important than a cat; she saves her sister. And she does this not by some mediocre act of heroism but by the ultimate act of heroism—sacrificing herself.

Act 1 is all about Katniss's and Peeta's training for the games at the Capitol and their mentoring by Haymitch. Here we see what the two are up against in terms of their opposition.

The turning point leading from Act 1 to Act 2 is when the tributes are transported through a glass tube to the surface where the Hunger Games begin. (See page 16 for an explanation of the games.)

Act 2 is all about the games—the bloodbath at the Cornucopia, the strategies, the alliances, the killings, the day-to-day survival.

The turning point leading from Act 2 to Act 3 is a little harder. Possibly, but I'm not sure, it is the announcement that there can be two winners instead of one, but only if the two come from the same district. This allows the storyline of the budding romance between Katniss and Peeta to continue, uniting them against the strongest tribute who has triumphed over all the others.

This alliance leads to the climax where Katniss saves Peeta's life by sending an arrow into the tribute who threatens to kill him.

In the denouement—the final scenes where the story is wrapped up—Katniss and Peeta are the heroes of the Hunger Games, inspirational role models who give hope to the 12 districts.

With that overview in mind, I begin scribbling down the spiritual parallels.

Okay, there's the Christ figure, Katniss, substituting herself for her sister. No-brainer. Then there's Peeta. Bound to be something in the bread he shares with her. A metaphor certainly. And who could miss that great scene where Donald Sutherland talks about hope?

I jot down a few ideas.

Reflect on them.

Scratch them out.

Jot some more.

Reflect.

Scratch out some more.

Then I realize . . .

I got nuthin'.

Zip.

Nada.

There were no references to God, no prayers to him, no talk of him—however hushed. There were no remains of our religious past—not the ruins of a church, not the fragment of a revered icon, not so much as a shard of stained glass.

Which puzzled me.

This was North America, after all. At least, "the ruins of a place once known as North America." There should have been something, somewhere.

There was nothing, anywhere.

A flashback from one of my classes in seminary comes to me, and I remember the book of Esther. Nowhere in the book is God mentioned. There are no prayers offered. No sacrifices. Scriptures are not quoted. Biblical images are not alluded to. Nothing. I remember the professor talking about how scholars debated over the book and whether it should be included in the canon of Scripture because of these omissions.

Then the professor's words came back to me: "God is conspicuous in his absence."

God was nowhere in the book; yet, at the same time, he was everywhere. The analogy is from C. S. Lewis, who said that God is in his creation the way Shakespeare is in his plays. He is nowhere in *Macbeth*; yet at the same time, he is everywhere. In every scene, every character, every line of dialogue.

That was it!

I start scribbling. Scratching out, scribbling on.

Good vs. evil. President Snow, played by Donald Sutherland, is a great image of Satan, working behind the scenes. And the character representing God? Let's see. Mm?

Haymitch maybe? He's at work behind the scenes, too. He watches over them, sends Katniss the ointment that heals her wound . . . sends her the note . . . and . . . and, eh . . .

I got nuthin'.

THE SEMINAL PRECURSORS TO THE STORY

Interview with Suzanne Collins
http://youtu.be/zUTPQCYVZEQ
1 minute, 14 seconds

God is nowhere in the film . . . a rather unsettling conclusion if it is your job to find him there.

So I went to the library to find him on the Internet. Surely the author must have said something about his conspicuous absence. But the author, I discovered, was herself conspicuously absent.

I began the way an archaeologist excavates an ancient site that had been buried by the sand of centuries. I sifted through the debris layers, finding shards here and there, a scrap of parchment now and then. Piece by piece the remains told a story.

The author *had* done a handful of interviews, I discovered, most of which were posted on her publisher's website. Like the one above. On that website she shared her inspiration for the series.

She was watching television one night, she explained, flipping through the channels with the remote, as we all do . . .

Click.

And she paused on a reality show. . . as many of us do. Let's face it—it's hard *not* to watch. It's hard not to get caught up in the drama, even though we know the drama is contrived.

I mean, how many times in life is a bachelorette given the opportunity to select a good-looking eligible bachelor from a bumper crop of good-looking eligible bachelors, each vying for her affection? With a huge production budget that allows her to be chauffeured in stretch limos on the most romantic dates and jetted away on the most exotic vacations. With a dressed-to-kill wardrobe. Complete with a stylist. A hairdresser. And a makeup artist.

Or how often are we marooned on some deserted island, left to survive by our wits and the strategic alliances we have forged? It's amazing what people will do, not for a million dollars, but just to be in the arena where winning a million dollars is possible. Of course, it is only possible if you are the last man standing. Or the last woman.

It's an interesting social phenomenon, and an equally interesting social commentary. These shows picture humanity at its best, and its worst. At its most generous, and its greediest. At its smartest, and its dumbest.

And we can't stop watching.

One wonders why.

At least, Suzanne Collins wondered. She reflected on what these reality shows revealed about our culture, and every one of us within that culture. But before she did, she reached for the remote.

Click.

Blazing across the television screen was footage from the war in Iraq. So many of the soldiers were so young. Barely out of high school. Teenagers, many of them. This was no reality show; it *was* reality. The battle was real, the bullets were real, the casualties were real. No one was voted out of the conflict to be driven home in some chauffeur-driven limousine. If these soldiers returned home, it was likely to be in a flag-draped coffin. And if you were lucky enough to be standing when the battle was over, there was no million-dollar prize waiting for you. You likely had to live the rest of your life with post-traumatic stress crippling your days and the horrors of war haunting your nights.

Then, with the suddenness of a click on the remote, it came to her. The ultimate reality show. A fight-to-the-death competition. Broadcast on television for all to see.

The Hunger Games!

O›

To refresh your memory, here is a summary of the film, which in places is a little different than the book. (If you are interested in the differences, I have a website in the Endnotes that lists them.)

Panem (the Latin word for *bread*) was once the prosperous land of North America and is the setting for the story. The political and economic collapse of the continent had been brought about by years of disasters, droughts, floods, and fires, followed by a devastating war that the country never recovered from.

A totalitarian regime rose from the ruins. Its center of power was called simply "The Capitol," the prosperous hub of a commercial wheel with spokes in all directions, dividing the land into sectors known as the 12 districts. There had been 13, but the thirteenth was blown to oblivion by a nuclear bomb after the rebellion.

As a way of reminding the people of the consequences of rebellion, the Capitol held an annual televised event called the Hunger Games. This year was the Seventy-Fourth Hunger Games. Each district sent two players, known as tributes, to participate in the games—one boy and one girl, chosen by lottery from a pool of 12 to 18 year olds.

This year, Katniss Everdeen, a 16-year-old girl from District 12, the coal mining district, goes with her 12-year-old sister Primrose to the "Reaping," where the lottery takes place.

At the Reaping, a cartoonish woman, played by Elizabeth Banks, makes the introductory remarks to the eligible children from that district.

EFFIE TRINKET
(speaking into a microphone)
Welcome! Welcome! Welcome! Happy Hunger Games!
And may the odds be ever in your favor.
Now, before we begin, we have a very special film brought to
     you all the way from the Capitol.

The film flashes images on a massive outdoor screen. The images are broadcast to all the districts, with footage of devastating droughts that destroy crops, ravenous seas that swallow coastal cities, isolated incidents of looting and rioting that froth into a collective rebellion. As jarring images of carnage fill the screen, a calm, reassuring voice speaks over the footage.

PRESIDENT SNOW

War, terrible war. Widows, orphans, a motherless child.

This was the uprising that rocked our land.

Thirteen districts rebelled against the country that fed them,
    loved them, protected them. Brother turned on brother
    until nothing remained.

And then came the peace, hard fought, sorely won.

The people rose up from the ashes and a new era was born.

But freedom has a cost and the traitors were defeated.

We swore as a nation we would never know this treason again.

And so it was decreed, that each year, the various districts
    of Panem would offer up in tribute, one young man
    and woman, to fight to the death in a pageant of honor,
    courage and sacrifice.

The lone victor, bathed in riches, would serve as a reminder
    of our generosity and our forgiveness.

Then, almost as a benediction, the voice says:

This is how we remember our past.

This is how we safeguard our future.

Then the drawing. In an unexpected twist of fate, Primrose's name is drawn from the fishbowl. As the terrified girl is ushered to the front, Katniss jumps out of line and volunteers to take her place.

The next name drawn is the boy who will represent the district—Peeta Mellark, the quiet baker's son who had once given bread to Katniss when she was shivering in the rain.

Both are transported to the Capitol for training on a luxurious railroad car, where they meet their mentor, a cynical alcoholic named Haymitch Abernathy. Once at the Capitol, they are fed and groomed and trained for battle. The Capitol is a garish collection of bizarre people, brought up living in excess, from the outlandish clothes they wear to the buffoonish way they shuffle from one extravagance to another.

During a televised interview, which is supposed to garner popular support and financial sponsorship, Peeta reveals his long-standing feelings for Katniss. This endears him to the crowd but enrages Katniss, who believes it is simply a ploy to leverage support. But it is no ploy.

Once the games begin, there is a bloodbath at the Cornucopia, the place where tributes can go to get food, water, and medicine, along with weapons. Almost killed in the melee, Katniss sprints away and keeps running until she is far from the field of battle.

By the end of the first day, half the tributes are dead. In the meantime, Peeta has formed an alliance with the career tributes, those who have trained their whole lives for a chance in the arena. Together they hunt down Katniss, who is hiding in a tree, having developed an alliance of sorts with Rue, the youngest of the tributes, hailing from District 11.

Peeta and the Careers, as they are called, spot Katniss in the tree. After several failed attempts to kill her, they decide to spend the night under her tree so she can't get away. During this time, Rue motions that there is a tracker jacker nest above her, which Katniss manages to dislodge, making it fall on the sleeping tributes. Fearing the deadly sting of this biologically engineered wasp, each of them flee for their lives.

Thinking it safe, Katniss and Rue climb down from their respective trees, where Katniss shares her food and her friendship, reassuring the young girl. Rue reminds her of Primrose, so young, so innocent, so helpless amid all these trained killers.

One such killer emerges from the woods and wounds Rue as Katniss shoots an arrow into him. But it is too late. Rue's life is ebbing away. In a tender moment, Katniss sings Rue a lullaby. Rue dies, and Katniss spreads flowers over her body. All of District 11 sees this on television. Collectively, they extend a grateful gesture to Katniss, then riot in the streets.

President Snow talks to Seneca, the Head Gamemaker, in his rose garden. Snow plucks a white rose from the bush and smells it, wanting to impart wisdom to the younger, less experienced man.

PRESIDENT SNOW
Seneca, why do you think we have a winner?
If we just wanted to intimidate the districts,
why not round up twenty-four of them at random
and execute them all at once?

Seneca is at a loss for words.

PRESIDENT SNOW

Hope. It's the only thing stronger than fear.
But it's also delicate. It can get out of control. Like a fire.
A little hope is effective. A lot of hope is dangerous.
The spark is fine as long as it is contained.

In an attempt to avoid further riots, the Gamemakers, realizing that these young lovers have become a crowd favorite, announce a rule change: two tributes can share the win, if they are from the same district. This gives hope to Katniss. To Peeta. To all the 12 districts.

Hearing this, Katniss scours the woods for Peeta, who has been wounded by a sword and is near death. She cares for him in the shelter of a cave, but she realizes he needs medicine. Risking her life to get it, she is almost killed by another tribute, but the male tribute from District 11 saves her because of what she did for Rue.

On her way back, Katniss comes across the body of the vicious girl tribute, Foxface, who has died from eating poisonous berries she had stolen from Peeta.

To make the game more interesting, the Gamemakers release a pack of overgrown, mutant hounds. Katniss and Peeta race to the safety of the Cornucopia, scrabble up a metal structure, away from the hounds' ravenous jaws . . . only to see Cato there, the strongest and meanest of the Careers; his face, bloodied; his eyes, smoldering cauldrons of hate. Muscling his arms around Peeta's neck, he taunts Katniss to shoot him. If she does, though, Peeta will fall to the ground, where the hounds will tear him to pieces.

After an intense struggle, Katniss seizes the opportunity and takes her shot. As Cato falls, he releases Peeta. The dogs fight over the body. Katniss shoots Cato again, mercifully putting him out of his misery.

It appears the Games are over, but over the loudspeakers comes an announcement. The rules have changed again. The judges have decided— only one winner. The hope, of course, is that the lovers will turn against each other in a dramatic fight to the finish.

Katniss takes some of the poisonous berries and puts them in Peeta's hand. She can't kill Peeta, and she knows that he can't kill her. So if there can't be two winners, there will be none. Just before that fateful decision, however, the Gamemakers declare them both winners.

The two are celebrated at the Capitol, and it seems to all to be the best Hunger Games ever. To everyone except President Snow. As they return to District 12, heroes, we are left with the ominous feeling that troubles him—that perhaps he has given the districts too much hope.

Rebellion is in the air. He can sense it.

And he fears not being able to contain it.

In another one of her video interviews, Collins talks about the classical influences that shaped her story. One was from ancient Rome; the other from ancient Greece.

The Roman gladiatorial games fascinated Collins. Barbarism in the midst of civilization. The two seemed at odds with each other. Yet they existed side by side for centuries. She explains how in one of her interviews (http://www.scholastic.com/thehungergames/videos/classical-inspiration.htm). For the gladiatorial games to arise in a civilized society, three things were needed:

One—a ruthless, all-powerful society.

Two—people who were forced to fight to the death.

Three—popular entertainment enjoyed by the masses.

And so, when the author started shaping her story, she structured those three things into it.

The other classical influence came from Greek mythology. As a child, one myth in particular stayed with her, influencing the shaping of *The Hunger Games.*

The Greek myth was the story of Theseus and the Minotaur. In the myth, King Aegeus of Athens had been defeated by Minos, the King of Crete, and was forced to pay tribute to him. As long as Aegeus paid the tribute, Minos agreed not to invade him.

The tribute consisted of seven young men and seven young women, chosen by lot. Minos offered them to the Minotaur, a powerfully savage beast with the head of a human and the body of a bull. The tributes were thrown one by one into an elaborately constructed labyrinth where the Minotaur lived. The screams coming from the labyrinth were terrifying. And the screams didn't stop until all 14 of the tributes had been devoured.

Determined to rid his countrymen of this threat, King Aegeus's only son, Theseus, offered himself as one of the victims. His plan? To slay the Minotaur. In spite of his father's protests, Theseus set sail for Crete. Greeted by King Minos, the tributes were honored at a festive banquet, as was his custom, giving them a sumptuous last meal.

The king's daughter, Ariadne, sat next to the handsome Theseus and was immediately taken with him, his strength, his courage. He told her that if she helped him, he would take her back to Athens and marry her. She agreed. Ariadne was to give Theseus a ball of silken thread. As he walked about the labyrinth, she was to unwind the thread so that he could go back through the maze without getting lost.

As Theseus crept through the darkness, sword in hand, he could hear the Minotaur sleeping with labored breath. Coming closer to the beast, Theseus woke him with a start. The Minotaur was a terrifying sight, and Theseus dropped his sword.

Regaining his composure, though, Theseus grabbed his sword and thrust it into the beast, killing it. Then he simply followed the string back through the labyrinth. After that, he set sail for home, where he was hailed a hero and ruled as a benevolent monarch.

The parallels are obvious.

Crete is the Capitol.

King Minos to President Snow.

The labyrinth is the arena.

The sending of young people to be sacrificed to the Minotaur parallels the sending of tributes to be sacrificed in the Hunger Games.

Theseus finds a parallel in Katniss, the one who, though the odds are decidedly not in her favor, defeats her enemies, winning her freedom and the right to go home. And like Theseus, she goes home a hero.

But there is something different about this hero.

And it isn't that she is a girl.

THE STRONG PROTAGONIST IN THE STORY

The Five Faces of Katniss
http://youtu.be/svul1d8SYpo
1 minute, 30 seconds

We need heroes, even superheroes. Maybe *especially* superheroes. I don't mean the ones in comic books with superpowers but rather the ones in combat boots with warfare skills.

Navy SEALS, for example.

Whether they are hunting down terrorists in hiding or rescuing hostages on the high seas, they work as a team—willing to go anywhere, anytime, and pay any cost to accomplish strategic missions.

The 2012 movie *Act of Valor,* written by Kurt Johnstad, shows such a team of warriors and the sacrifices they make to keep our country safe from terrorists. They are the best of the best. They have the best character, the best training, the best skills, the best weapons, and the best technology available to them. They are sent to be invisible and to do the impossible.

The night before Seal Team 7 leaves for a special op, the men are at the beach with their families. Standing around a campfire, one of them makes a toast to his team: "To us, and those like us—damn few."

We, the many, need those few. We need them not simply for the missions they accomplish but for the examples they furnish.

We need a David, for instance. And we need his mighty men. "Men of valor," as they were known, 30 of the best warriors in Israel's army. And the three captains over them were the best of the best. Here are their names and the missions they accomplished:

> These are the names of the mighty men whom David had: Josheb-basshebeth a Tachemonite, chief of the captains, he was called Adino the Eznite, because of eight hundred slain by him at one time; and after him was Eleazar the son of Dodo the Ahohite, one of the three mighty men with David when they defied the Philistines who were gathered there to battle and the men of Israel had withdrawn. He arose and struck the Philistines until his hand was weary and clung to the sword, and the LORD brought a great victory that day; and the people returned after him only to strip the slain.
>
> Now after him was Shammah the son of Agee a Hararite. And the Philistines were gathered into a troop where there was a plot of ground full of lentils, and the people fled from the Philistines. But he took his stand in the midst of the plot, defended it and struck the Philistines; and the LORD brought about a great victory. (2 Samuel 23:8–12, NASB)

Israel had its women heroes, too. Rahab, Deborah, and Esther, to name a few. When Israel was terrorized for 20 years by the Canaanite army, led by Sisera, the leader of Israel's army came to Deborah for counsel.

> Now Deborah, a prophetess, the wife of Lappidoth, was judging Israel at that time. She used to sit under the palm tree of Deborah between Ramah and Bethel in the hill country of Ephraim; and the sons of Israel came up to her for judgment.
>
> Now she sent and summoned Barak the son of Abinoam from Kedesh-naphtali, and said to him, "Behold, the LORD, the God of Israel, has commanded, 'Go and march to Mount Tabor, and take with you ten thousand men from the sons of Naphtali and from the sons of Zebulun. I will draw out to you Sisera, the commander of Jabin's army, with his chariots and his many troops to the river Kishon, and I will give him into your hand.'" (Judges 4:4–7, NASB)

The commander of Israel's army looked up to Deborah so much that he drew confidence from her, so much so that he said to her: "If you will go with me, then I will go; but if you will not go with me, I will not go" (v. 8).

Like David's warriors, Deborah was a person of valor.

The Hebrew word for *valor* is *chayíl* (pronounced *kah-yeel,* accent on the second syllable), taken from the verb *chíl* (pronounced *keel*). The verbal root means "to be firm or strong." It is a word used to describe warriors. But not just any warriors. Super warriors.

> From the Gadites there came over to David in the stronghold in the wilderness, mighty men of *valor*, men trained for war, who could handle shield and spear, and whose faces were like the faces of lions, and they were as swift as the gazelles on the mountains. (1 Chronicles 12:8, NASB, italics mine)

The word *valor* is also used to describe women in the Bible. It is used of Ruth (Ruth 3:11), and it is also used of the "woman of excellence" in Proverbs 12:4 and 31:10–31. The phrase could be translated the "strong woman" or the "valiant woman," even the "exceptional woman," for the idea is one of exceptional strength, exceptional character, and exceptional skill.

We need those kinds of heroes, male and female.

We need our Deborahs as well as our Davids, our Katnisses as well as our Peetas. But we don't need our Deborahs *to be* Davids, or our Katnisses *to be* Peetas. We don't need competing heroes but rather complementary heroes.

In the *USA Today* article, "Film Females Join the Fight Club," Susan Wloszczyna, writes:

> In the past, woman action heroes tended to come in two varieties: seductive supervixen (Angelina Jolie as Lara Croft, Pam Grier as Foxy Brown) or macho tomboy (Carrie-Anne Moss as Trinity in *The Matrix*, Kiera Knightley as Domino). Their intended targets? Young male moviegoers whose libidinous fantasies often seem to involve skintight leather.

Then along comes Katniss Everdeen, who is neither supervixen nor tomboy.

She is attractive, but plainly so. Her beauty is simple and unadorned. Her eyes, not hard at all, but you can tell her life has been hard. She is confident but not arrogant. She is used to hard work, yet there is a softness to her. She is used to getting her hands dirty as she forages in the forest, but she uses those same hands to hold her little sister on her lap. She is used to gutting the animals she has killed to feed her family, but, as Lawrence is quick to point out in a November 2, 2011, interview with Krista Smith of *Vanity Fair,* Katniss is "a hunter but not a killer." Yes, she kills in the games, but only in self-defense or in order to save someone else from being killed. She takes no joy in it, as some of the other tributes do.

She is one tough woman.

But she is also a tender woman.

She shoots an arrow through the tribute that kills Rue, for instance, but she also carefully picks flowers and gracefully arranges them on Rue's grave, afterwards sobbing by herself in the forest.

In the film, we see the range of Katniss's attributes, each showing a different aspect of her strength. She is—as the film clip at the beginning of the chapter reveals—sister, tribute, archer, lover, and the girl on fire. The author who first envisioned Katniss in the book and the actor who finally portrayed her in the film created a female character we haven't really seen before. We've seen strong women in film roles, but this one is different. Peter Travers, writing for the *Rolling Stone,* stated it best. In his March 21 review of the movie, he writes that Katniss "gives us a female warrior worth cheering."

The image of the "female warrior" is closer to the biblical image of a woman than the ones we see displayed on magazine racks in the grocery stores. I'm thinking of Genesis 2:18, where "the Lord God said, 'It is not good that man should be alone; I will make him a helper comparable to him'" (NASB).

The Hebrew word translated *helper* is *ezer* (pronounced *etz-air,* accent on the second syllable). It has been interpreted a number of ways over the millennia, but the most common interpretation has been to view the woman as subordinate to the man in a way that undermines her equality.

But that is not the original meaning of the word. It is so much richer than that. It is used some 80 times in the Old Testament. When you look at the passages where the word is used, two things stand out.

One, it is used primarily in military contexts.

And two, it is used primarily of God.

The word has the same meaning in all the language families that are closely related to Hebrew. It means "to rescue" or "to save." The sense of the word is of a military ally who comes to fight by our side when we are under attack. This is how it is used in Psalm 46. The psalm shows a future picture of the world in upheaval, a time when Jerusalem is surrounded by enemies that threaten to destroy her. In the midst of this impending attack, the psalmist declares:

> There is a river whose streams shall make glad the city of God, the holy place of the tabernacle of the Most High. God is in the midst of her, she shall not be moved; God shall *help* her, just at the break of dawn. The nations raged, the kingdoms were moved; He uttered His voice, the earth melted (vv. 4–6, NKJV, italics mine).

Psalm 46 uses the same word Genesis 2 uses. Rescuer, savior, ally. A special creation, patterned after divinity. A special force, exceptional in every way. A feminine force, secure enough to be tough without surrendering her tenderness. A valiant warrior, worth cheering.

In preparation for her role in the film, Jennifer Lawrence was taught archery by an Olympian. In this year's summer games (2012), for the first time in Olympic history, women athletes on the U.S. team outnumbered the men. So did their medals. Twenty-nine of our 46 gold medals were won by women.

I like what the Bible says about those women. And I like what Susan Wloszczyna says about them in *USA Today*: "The next time someone says you fight like a girl, consider it a compliment."

PART II

The Contemporary Story

What history has shown us is that a state of decadence simply
cannot last. Invariably such a society collapses.

Adrienne Kress
"The Inevitable Decline of Decadence"

THE SOCIAL PHENOMENON OF THE STORY

ABC News: Premiere of the Movie
http://abcnews.go.com/GMA/video/hunger-games-premiere-cast-red-carpet-15908650
2 minutes, 5 seconds

In the summer of 1999, I attended a month-long intensive in Los Angeles to help prepare Christian writers for careers in screenwriting. The program was called "Act One." While I was there, I remember walking to an intersection, where I stopped to wait for the light to change. As I waited, my eyes caught a bit of graffiti scratched into the back of a sign. It read: *All I learned about life I learned from John Hughes' films.*

I remember smiling when I read it, thinking back over some of his films I had seen and also learned from—*Sixteen Candles* (1984), *The Breakfast Club* (1985), *Ferris Bueller's Day Off* (1986).

Okay, I didn't learn that much from *Ferris Bueller's Day Off*. I had already mastered the art of skipping class while in college, so much so, in fact, I could have made my own movie. Maybe what I did learn from the film was that my truancies weren't so much character flaws as they were fairly common dalliances that most kids experience along the way to growing up.

That bit of graffiti gives a clue to why we go to the movies, why we all go to the movies. So does a bit of wisdom from Robert McKee, legendary screenwriting teacher whose seminar on *Story* I also attended in Los Angeles. In his book by the same title, he writes: "A storyteller is a life poet, an artist who transforms day-to-day living, inner life and outer life, dream and actuality into a poem whose rhyme scheme is events rather than words—a two-hour metaphor that says: Life is like *this!"*

We go to the movies for a lot of reasons: to take our own *Day Off,* perhaps, and escape our lives for a couple of hours; to experience the thrill of the roller coaster ride that is an action film, because, let's face it, the drone of daily life can get pretty dull; or to enjoy a comedy, because God knows we all carry such heaviness inside us that we need a little laughter now and then to lighten the load.

One of the reasons we go to the movies, though, is to learn about life. We learn about life in general and about our own lives in particular through the images that flicker in the dark and linger long after we leave the theater. Through the truth of other people's stories we sometimes glimpse something of the truth of our own. Something of the joy of our own. Or the sadness of our own. Something of the uniqueness of our story. Or the sameness of our story with the stories of others. Something of its sacredness, too, which we can't see so well in the light, but which sparkles in the darkness.

For better or worse, we get a lot of our social cues from the movies. We may learn how to kiss, how to dance, how to dress, all from the movies— sometimes all from *one* movie. We may learn how to smoke in a way that looks cool, or we may learn that it isn't that cool to smoke, no matter how we do it. We may learn the secret lives of teachers (who knew?) or the secret of surviving middle school. We may learn about the pleasures of sex, or the pain of sex. We may learn about good and evil, especially the good and evil that lives in us. We may learn that "might makes right" . . . or we may learn that "might for right" is a far nobler idea upon which to build a civilization.

Which brings us back to the social phenomenon of the film.

Why did we go to the theater, you and I? Why did others go by the millions, young and old?

We went mostly because we loved the book. This raises perhaps a more poignant question: What did we take with us when we left?

Images. Larger-than-life. Looming not only on the silver screen but somewhere in the theater of our subconscious.

Stark images from the districts. Bizarre images from the Capitol. Violent images from the arena. Images of selfishness. Images of sacrifice. Images of what we fear we might say when our backs are against the wall, might do when the odds are against us, might become if the Gamemakers have their way with us. But there are also other images in the film—images of what we long with all our hearts to say to someone we love; what we long with all our hearts to do in life, even if it will cost us our lives; what we long with all our hearts to become, if only we have the courage not to let the games change who we are.

Those images inform us, inspire us, and are more important than ever, because we live in a world no longer driven by character but by image.

The pressures imposed by a society that emphasizes image over character have led to other social phenomena—compulsive dieting, substance abuse, anorexia, bulimia, depression. Even suicide. Children killing children. Only this time it's themselves they are killing. And often it's because they don't like the image they see in the mirror or the image they see reflected in the Facebook posts from their classmates.

How did we get where we are today, where perfecting and protecting our image has become the driving force of our survival?

Cultural critic Os Guinness offers this explanation:

> Over the last century and a half, life has moved from the country to cities, and from small, stable, face-to-face relationships to fast, superficial, largely anonymous acquaintances. The result is an accompanying shift from an emphasis on internal character to one's external appearance. Thus the traditional ideal of "the strong character" has given way to "the striking personality" and "the successful image." In a world in which first impressions may be all there is, plastic surgery is as natural a response as press agents, spin doctors, and *People* magazine.

When the emphasis of our culture shifted from character to image, institutions aimed at developing character declined and institutions aimed at creating images emerged. These were largely media institutions like television, movies, magazines, advertising. As a result, the character-developing role of parents, teachers, and ministers was eclipsed by the image-creating role of screen idols, fashion models, and pop icons. Advertising firms, marketing departments, and a babel of consultants came together to create and perpetuate these images.

And what have those images cost?

Our truest, deepest, most beautiful self.

That is what Peeta fears it may cost him. One night before the games, he and Katniss are talking inside a building overlooking the Capitol, where they can hear the muffled cheers of the crowd outside.

KATNISS

Listen to them.

PEETA

Yeah. I just hope they don't change me.

KATNISS

How would they change you?

PEETA

I don't know. Turn me into something I'm not. Another piece
in their game, you know.

KATNISS

You mean you won't kill anyone?

PEETA

No. I'm sure I would, just like anyone else.

You know, I just keep wishing I could think of a way to show
them they don't own me. You know, if I'm gonna die, I
wanna still be me.

Peeta is afraid, not so much of dying but of something within him dying. There is something he's holding on to, something that lies at the core of who he is, defining who he is. And that, above all, is what he wants to survive. We are all fashioned in the image of God, made in his likeness. That, I think, is what Peeta is holding on to, though he doesn't use those words.

If God is anywhere in *The Hunger Games,* he is there. Something of his image can be glimpsed in moments like this. Something of his likeness can be seen in Peeta and in Katniss throughout the film, mostly in little acts of kindness: in bread that is shared, or a song; in a hug, or a smile; in sharing their soup, a spoonful at a time, or their feelings, a story at a time.

In this tender sharing of Peeta's feelings, it is the image of God in him that is crying out. Whenever that image gets defaced, it resists the hand responsible for the damage. It cries out when we are marginalized or made to feel less than who we have been created to be. It cries out when we are used, made to feel like a commodity that can be bought and sold. It doesn't matter the game, whether it is sports or sex. It doesn't matter the arena, whether in the National Football League or the local junior league. Any game in any arena has the power to change a person, either to crush that image or to corrupt it.

The first casualty in those games is the humanity of its participants. And that is what Peeta fears most—not losing his life but losing himself. In playing the game, he fears that what makes him uniquely who he is will either be corrupted beyond recognition or else crushed beyond recognition.

Peeta also understands the power of the games to manipulate people's images in order to sway public opinion. We do too, don't we? Remember the exchange between Katniss and her fashion consultant, Cinna? She thinks he is there to make her look pretty. But he is there to help her make an impression.

Why is making an impression so important? Because it is how the game is played. It's what gets you sponsors and ratings, which are what keep you alive. Those words from Cinna echo the ones our society speaks to us, either explicitly or implicitly.

We feel as if we are in an arena, thrust into a savage game where we either have to kill or be killed. Everyone is watching, and we feel we must do whatever it takes to win. Socially. Academically. Vocationally. Financially. A lot is at stake. If we win, we get the scholarship or the membership, the job or the promotion, the friendships or the romance we desire. And so we must make the impression that will gain us sponsorships and get us ratings so that the odds may be ever in our favor.

If we have to change how we look, how we act, what we say or don't say, it's a small price to pay, isn't it?

Besides, it's only an image we are changing, not who we are.

Not who we really are.

O)

We live at a time where images dominate the landscape of our lives, not only in movie theaters but also outside them. I remember taking a walk one night down the higher numbered streets of Sunset Boulevard, craning my neck at the intensely lighted billboards. One of the advertisers had an image of a drop-dead gorgeous young woman in an evening dress. I have long since forgotten the words in the ad, but not the image. Calvin Klein had a cut image of a young man in his underwear. Entire walls of buildings were used as advertising space. One had a several-stories-high image of Halle Berry, if I remember correctly, highlighting her upcoming film about the life of Dorothy Dandridge. It all was so surreal, as if I were walking through some glittering pantheon of Roman gods and goddesses.

The images were spellbinding.

Even *I* wanted that underwear.

That is the power of images. They seduce us into wanting them or wanting the world they inhabit. Images that move are especially seductive. When we look at moving images in film, we project them in our minds, consciously or subconsciously, as role models. Only 16, and already Katniss Everdeen has inspired a generation of young filmgoers, whose role models predominately have been celebrities emblazoning the covers of glamour magazines. Or poised on red carpets. Or parading on catwalks. Or placed on some other media pedestal with a strobe of camera shutters, capturing their images.

Like the propaganda film shown by the Capitol during the Reaping of District 12, though, the images distort reality. Many of them, in fact, are airbrushed by technicians who manipulate the images. Taking a little off the thighs. Adding a little to the breasts. Covering up the blemishes on the face. Photoshopping the color in the eyes.

The magazine images are of rising stars, mostly, stylishly photographed on glossy paper. The tabloid images are mostly of falling stars, photographed without makeup, their hair a mess, their eyes bloodshot from a night of partying, to serve as a cautionary tale told in newsprint that rubs off on your hands, leaving you feeling a little smudged for having read them.

If you are looking for a role model, these aren't great options to choose from. That is why Jennifer Lawrence's portrayal of Katniss has become something of a social phenomenon. People are taking archery classes because of her. And that is not all they are taking. They are taking social cues from her, even vocational cues.

In a world obsessed with beauty, image is everything. Image is everything to God, as well, only in a different way. In Genesis 1:27, we read: "So God created mankind in his own image, in the image of God he created them; male and female he created them."

The image of a ruler was often erected on the borders of the ruler's kingdom to announce to anyone entering it who he was, how powerful he was, and the extent of the territory over which he reigned. It was a billboard of sorts towering over the landscape to inspire awe in all who saw it.

What is significant about the Genesis passage is it states that the image of God is made up of male *and* female. In other words, there is a masculine side of God, but that is only half of who he is. There is also a feminine side—some say the better half—without which, your image of God will be a distorted one.

Even though the masculine pronoun is used of God, along with masculine descriptions such as Father, feminine images are sometimes ascribed to him. In Isaiah 49:14–15, for example, the image used to describe God's relationship with us is that of a mother to her nursing child. In Matthew 23:37, another image is used, that of a mother hen gathering her chicks under her wings.

The blending of these characteristics is beautifully pictured in the parable of the prodigal son in Luke 15. The decision to let the younger son leave is more of a masculine response to a rebellious child. I'm not sure a woman would have done that. But when the son returns, the father's actions are more of a feminine response. He runs to the boy, showers him with kisses and hugs, gets him fresh clothes, and throws a party for him. I'm not sure a man would have done that.

What we have in the parable is as clearly developed a picture of God as we seen anywhere in the Scriptures, which is a wonderful union of masculine and feminine qualities. What we have in Jennifer Lawrence's interpretation of Katniss Everdeen is also a wonderful union of masculine and feminine qualities. She isn't exactly Eve, but she is a whole lot closer to the biblical image of a woman than you will see in most movies or magazines.

Speaking of which . . .

Jennifer Lawrence was on the April 2012 cover of *Glamour*, looking pretty—glamorous. I didn't see the magazine until after I had seen the film. When I thumbed through the pages to get to her interview, I was struck by how different the magazine images were from the movie images. In one of the full-page photos, she is dressed like a seductress in black tights with a neckline that plunges to her waist. She is standing with a bow in front of her, hips slightly to one side, windblown hair, and a look on her face as if she might actually enjoy hunting men.

It's all staged, of course, with a lighting crew along with a wind machine and someone to operate it, a photographer posing her, a designer dressing her, a makeup artist blushing her cheeks, a stylist mussing her hair, a post-production artist, and a team of editors poring over the images.

I doubt the editors saw the movie before the photo shoot. If they had, they would have seen the irony.

One hopes, anyway.

Regardless, the magazine's images didn't create the social phenomenon. The movie's images did.

O>

Besides our need for images to shed light on who we are as human beings and to inspire us regarding who we might become, there is another reason for the social phenomenon of the film—our fears.

The world has become an increasingly scary place in which to live, and the people who went to the movie—especially those between 12 and 18—went to see just how scary it could get.

They are fearful about the future and their place in it. Not an uncommon anxiety for teenagers. When I was a teen, there was the Cold War and the threat of nuclear annihilation. What we are now seeing in the world is different, though—more ominous, more inevitable. The whole earth seems in upheaval, doesn't it? And doesn't that scare you? Not concern—*scare*.

Hurricanes. Wildfires. Floods. Earthquakes. Tsunamis. Record heat. Widespread drought. Famines. Civil wars. Cyber wars. The collapse of global economies, global ecosystems.

Could things *get* any worse?

The propaganda film shown at the Reaping answers that question with larger-than-life images of battle scenes and a mushroom cloud from an atomic bomb. . . .

Things *could* get worse.

Everything is not only scarier, everything is faster. It's impossible to keep up with the changes. It's impossible not to feel overwhelmed, not to feel as if the world is passing you by and leaving you in its dust. Here is just one example of how fast the world is changing.

Michael Mendelbaum coauthored the book, *That Used to Be Us,* with his friend Thomas Friedman, Pulitzer prize-winning author and columnist for *The New York Times.* It was published in 2011. In it, Mendelbaum writes:

> Since *The World Is Flat* was published in 2005, the world has only gotten, well, flatter. How far and how fast have we come? When Tom wrote *The World Is Flat,* Facebook wasn't even in it, "Twitter" was still a sound, the "cloud" was something in the sky, "3G" was a parking space, "applications" were what you sent to colleges, and "Skype" was a typo.

Those are a lot of changes in a short six years. Who can keep up with them?

Everything is not only faster, but shakier. Billions are made faster, that's true, but they are also lost faster. Not only have too-big-to-fail corporations failed, entire countries are on the brink of failing. We know what happens when a corporation goes bankrupt, but what happens when a country goes bankrupt?

The truth is, we don't really know.

It hasn't happened in a while, not to a major country anyway.

Could *The Hunger Games* show what our country will look like in the not-too-distant future?

Children killing children . . . at a high school in Columbine . . . in the inner city of Chicago.

Children killing children . . . with knives . . . with guns.

Children killing children . . . barely mothers, barely babies.

Children killing children . . . for drug money . . . Air Jordans even, if you can believe it.

We don't need a fortune-teller to show us the future; the future is here. And we're all speeding past concern, past afraid, careening off the emotional streets we know to destinations unknown.

We feel more and more paranoid. We try to reason with ourselves, talk ourselves out of our worst fears, but how can we not feel a little paranoid when surveillance cameras, just like those in *The Hunger Games,* are everywhere, tracking our every move? And if the cameras can't find us, our cell phones will give us up. And if our cell phones don't know where we are, our computers do. We are being watched, tracked, catalogued. There is a file on us somewhere of what we buy, where we buy it, and how often. It may take some sophisticated software to gather the information, but the information is there.

Cameras are giving us traffic tickets. *What's next?* we wonder. I have a Magellan GPS system in my car with the computer-generated voice of a woman, whose name is Maggie. Maggie calmly tells me where to turn and when, when to make a "legal" U-turn if I've missed my turn, and how far away that U-turn is—measured in feet. The voice also says, "WARNING" in a firm voice if I'm speeding. In a way, I appreciate that. In another way, I wonder if Maggie might one day rat me out to the police.

Another privacy invaded. Another freedom taken away. And we wonder, what else do "they" know? And will they use it against us? To raise our medical insurance, perhaps, or to cancel it.

That is another reason why the film resonated with so many, I think. It touches a chord, a chord in us that is already quivering.

Images of the districts also touch our fear. Many of us have seen newsreels of the Great Depression, soup lines stretching for blocks, bankers selling apples on the street, businesses wiped out, people out of work, out of hope. And the faces. Who could forget those faces? Foreheads furrowed with worry. Eyes bagged from fatigue. Heads downturned in shame.

The images of life in District 12 touch a chord with kids, too, most of whom have never seen images from the Depression.

Many are graduating college and going off not to start their careers but their night shift at a coffee shop. They have loans in the six figures, some of them, and the best they can get is minimum wage. They move home to save money, only to find that home is a different place than when they left it. It's tense now. Dad fears getting laid off after 20 years on the job, or fears being passed over by a workforce half his age, who will work for half his salary. Mom has two part-time jobs, but no benefits, and she's worried about what will happen if her husband loses his insurance.

Maybe that is why so many of us went to the film—to glimpse a future we fear is already upon us. To see how much worse it could get, and to see if we could survive it.

THE SOCIETAL PICTURES IN THE STORY

Interview with Father Robert Barron, Part II
http://youtu.be/VpCowqg_pHI
4 minutes, 41 seconds

The Hunger Games has parallels to a short story that first appeared in *The New Yorker* literary magazine on June 26, 1948, titled, "The Lottery," by Shirley Jackson.

The story takes place between ten in the morning and noon on a summer day in a small, New England town. People in the town meet in front of the post office for the annual lottery where everyone has to draw a folded slip of paper from a black box. When the drawing is complete, they open their slips of paper to see who has the one piece of paper with the black dot.

This year, Tessie Hutchinson's name is drawn.

Once the identity of this year's lottery winner is revealed, the rest of the people pick up rocks, close in on her, and stone her to death. After the stoning, people go about their business as if nothing has happened.

At the beginning of the story, the author foreshadows the horror that is to come:

> Bobby Martin had already stuffed his pockets full of stones,
> and the other boys soon followed his example, selecting
> the smoothest and roundest stones; Bobby and Harry
> Jones and Dickie Delacroix . . . eventually made a great
> pile of stones in one corner of the square and guarded it
> against the raids of the other boys.

Children draw from the black box and participate in the stoning, which perhaps is the most shocking thing about the story, especially the possibility of a lottery happening one day where children would be killing one of their own—a playmate perhaps, or a sibling.

Readers reacted with a stoning of their own, hurling sharp-edged complaints, many threatening to cancel their subscriptions. But when the dust settled, critics rallied to the story's defense. Their conclusion? It was shocking, yes, but socially relevant.

The civilization of *The Hunger Games* is different from the one in "The Lottery." In "The Lottery," the acceptance of the tradition is casual; in *The Hunger Games,* it is celebrated.

The parallels are obvious. Both stories speak of civilizations in decay. Sometimes the only way to reach such civilizations is to shock them. This is what *The Hunger Games* did.

That we *need* shocking is not a criticism of the storyteller. It is a criticism of the civilization to which the story is told.

When Augustus was emperor, Rome had a population of a quarter million. One of the ways the government garnered the support of its people was to buy it through a welfare program that started with Augustus. The poor within the city limits were given all the bread, oil, and wine they needed to sustain themselves. To sweeten the pot, free entertainment was thrown in.

The greatness of the Republic was, over the centuries, usurped by the corruption of the Caesars. Over time, the people became more interested in the gladiatorial battles than the battles on the frontier; more interested in their free food than in their freedom. The satirist Juvenal wrote of this sad state of affairs: "The people that once bestowed commands, consulships, legions, and all else, now concerns itself no more, and longs eagerly for just two things—bread and circuses."

As I mentioned before, the Latin word for *bread* is *panem,* the name of the land in *The Hunger Games* that was ruled by its own Caesar—President Snow. Like the Caesars of Rome, he controlled the Capitol by satiating the appetites of its populace. Life in the Capitol was one long, lavish Mardi Gras, patterned after the excesses of Rome during its decline. The games were staged on a grand scale, each met with grander and grander expectations of the audience. Chariot races were held in the Circus Maximus. Before long, though, the audience wanted more—bigger, better, bloodier. One such event was sponsored by the emperor Trajan, boasting 123 straight days of partying and games that featured a roster of 10,000 gladiators.

Entertainment became more extravagant and more violent. Exotic animals were paraded before the audience—elephants, lions, rhinoceroses, giraffes. Some were trained to do tricks. Others were hunted. Bigger and better hunts were choreographed—3,500 were killed in a series of festivals under Augustus; 9,000 were slaughtered in one day to celebrate the completion of the Colosseum in A.D. 80; 11,000 were killed over a four-month period in A.D. 107, celebrating a military victory.

Then there were the "blood sports," where armed men fought the animals, or where lions were starved and then sent into the arena to devour a victim tethered to a stake. The hunger for spectacle was insatiable. More games. More gore. It was an all-you-could-watch buffet, if you had the stomach for it.

Within a generation after Jesus was crucified, the Roman Emperor, Nero, staged a public execution at the Circus Maximus, an arena often used for chariot races. A fire had recently destroyed much of Rome, and someone had to be the scapegoat. Nero blamed Christians. Three thousand of them—men, women, and children—were rounded up and executed in the most savage of ways: burned alive on wooden crosses, eaten alive by wild animals, beaten to death, skewered to death, hacked to death. The stands were full of spectators. They came to the circus and received their bread. They ate, they drank. They watched, they cheered.

At the end of the day, they went home.

The next day, they went back to work. And the next. Until the hunger for their entitlements and their entertainment came back to them. Thus the games continued, unabated, year after bloody year, decade after brutal decade, century after barbaric century.

Until the fifth century.

O›

The Hunger Games pictures a society in the final stages of decay. Life in that society is lived under a dictatorship that exploits the outlying districts in order to satisfy the hungers of the Capitol—the hunger for bread and circuses.

When the high-speed train transports Katniss and Peeta to the Capitol, you are immediately struck by the excesses—from the food to the fashions. The games seem to be just another excess, something like the games of ancient Rome, where audiences sat in the Colosseum watching gladiators fight to their deaths.

In her essay, "Someone to Watch Over Me," Lili Wilkinson says,

> [A]lthough the Districts dread the reaping, all of Panem tunes to watch the Hunger Games as eagerly as we tune in to watch *Survivor* or *American Idol*. Why do they watch it? Do they really enjoy seeing their children murder each other? Why don't they refuse to watch? What would happen if every citizen of Panem just turned off the television?
>
> But nobody does. The viewers at home are just as bloodthirsty and eager for drama as we are when watching an episode of *The Bachelorette* or *The Amazing Race*. What does that say about the people of Panem? What does it say about the way they and their society are controlled? And what does it say about us?

This brings us to the story of a man who lived in the fifth century A.D. According to church historian Theodoret, Telemachus was a monk who felt God telling him to go to Rome. He wasn't told why, but this unassuming man with simple faith packed up what few belongings he had in a bag and set off for the imperial city.

Once in Rome, he became caught up in a crowd streaming into the entrance of the stadium. With the others, he took a seat in the stands. When the games began, gladiators paraded into the arena. The contests were savage, each one a fight to the death.

Telemachus was horrified by the barbarism he saw in the arena, but he was equally horrified at the crowd being entertained by it. They were on their feet, cheering their favorites, jeering the ones who weren't delivering a good show. Unable to reason with them, Telemachus jumped into the arena, stepping between two combatants, pleading with them to stop. The crowd was outraged. First, they threw obscenities, then they threw stones.

Telemachus fell to the ground, his blood ebbing out of him, staining the ground. And that is where he died—in the arena.

News of the incident came to the attention of the emperor, who immediately canceled the games. With that decree, killing as entertainment for the masses ceased. And that is how history chronicles the end of the gladiatorial games.

Sometimes it takes a good person dying before a society realizes how much of its soul has been lost in how its citizens entertain themselves. Sometimes it takes an innocent young Rue dying in the arena before we as an audience realize how much blood we have on our hands just by watching the games that are played there, games which, to some degree, are played everywhere, in one arena or another: in family feuds or in national debates; by bullies in schoolyards or bosses in boardrooms. Infighting or dogfighting. Political wars or ratings wars. Radio talk shows or cable news shows.

It is all so entertaining, so deliciously entertaining.

Until someone dies. Then the appetites that once drove us to watch, now drive us away.

There is a poignant moment between Gale and Katniss at the beginning of the movie. As they sit beside each other on a grassy hillside, a more somber Gale wonders why the districts couldn't simply stop watching. Without an audience, he reasons, there wouldn't be a game.

He makes a good point. We often blame Hollywood for what we see on television, but the truth is that networks simply provide what we have an appetite for. If there weren't an appetite for what is on the menu, the restaurant wouldn't be serving it.

Perhaps I am letting Hollywood off easy.

But if we do blame Hollywood for the obscenity in our society, do we blame McDonald's for the obesity?

PART III

The Coming Story

Therefore keep watch, because you do not know on what day
your Lord will come. But understand this: If the owner of
the house had known at what time of night the thief was
coming, he would have kept watch and would not have
let his house be broken into. So you also must be ready,
because the Son of Man will come at an hour when you
do not expect him.

Jesus
Matthew 24:42–44

THE SPIRITUAL PARALLELS IN THE STORY

Interview with Father Robert Barron, Part I
http://youtu.be/RsFBbS39_z0
10 minutes, 13 seconds

When I started doing research for this book, I came across a lot of insights on finding God in *The Hunger Games*, or on spiritual parallels in the film, Christ figures, stuff like that. But at the end of the day—granted, it was sometimes at the end of a bleary-eyed day—I didn't see what they saw.

It's not important why.

I did learn something, though. What I learned was that people on the Internet have strong opinions. *Really* strong. And they express them strongly. *Really* strongly. Some of the comments were downright hateful—mean, pins-in-a-voodoo-doll hateful; spit-in-your-face hateful. The people, a number of them Christians, it seemed, were smug and sarcastic and said things to people online they never would have said to them in person.

There was such arrogance in their tone, such condescension.

Do Christians really talk like that to their critics?

They just seemed so sure of themselves, so dig-in-their-heels certain that they were right and the other person had to have been some lunatic on furlough from the asylum to have come up with such incoherent babble.

Will Rogers once said: "Everyone is ignorant, only on different subjects."

Okay, maybe not Alex Trebek. But pick any other Alex you know, put him on *Jeopardy!*, and there's going to be some category that stumps him, some subject about which he is ignorant.

Here is where our hearts are put in jeopardy. Knowledge, the Bible says, has a tendency to puff us up rather than humble us. And that is true even of biblical knowledge. The truth, whatever any of us has of it, should fill us with humility and gratitude and joy, and our sharing of it should be like "one beggar telling another beggar where to find bread."

Christ believed that humility was a foundational virtue. The first beatitude in the Sermon on the Mount, for example, is "blessed are the poor in spirit" (Matthew 5:3). Confucius believed that too, by the way.

I don't want to put my own heart in jeopardy, but I really struggle with people who have an opinion on everything, who are convinced their opinions are right, who feel strongly that those opinions are the only ones that should be heard, and who have an almost evangelistic zeal in making them heard.

I would love to run into an intelligent, well-read Christian who said, "I don't know" now and then, or "I'm not sure" on something about which others seem so certain. Or, "I don't have all the facts and so I don't feel really qualified to judge." Or, "I've only heard one side all my life, so I'm a little biased, but I would love to hear another perspective."

Personal humility. Intellectual humility. Moral humility. It seems they shouldn't be separate strands of the same virtue but rather the same strand, so inextricably woven through the fabric of our being it would be impossible to touch on any subject without causing a corresponding tug from that part of our character.

We are all sinners, only in different areas. We live with, struggle with, and are addicted to different sins, you and I, sins that may be obvious to others but to which we perhaps are oblivious. Different sins we confess, or don't.

And maybe this is a good time and place to do that. To confess our sins, one to another. The list is long. And the confession, long overdue: "Bless us, Father, for we have sinned. It's been a thousand years since our last confession."

For the first three hundred years of its existence, Christianity was a blight upon the Roman Empire, with one Caesar after another determined to put an end to it. Then came Constantine, ruler of the empire, who saw a sign of the cross in the clouds (or so he claimed), assuring him that by this sign he would conquer. His conversion influenced his legislation, and in A.D.

315, he signed an edict not only ending three centuries of state-sponsored persecution but making Christianity the state religion.

When Christians gained political power, they used that power to raze pagan temples, slaughter their priests, and purge the empire of paganism, down to the last shard of it.

Each century increased its zealotry. By the eighth century, it was all-out war. Leading the charge was Charlemagne, whose battle cry was "Saxony must be Christianized, or wiped out."

The worst carnage took place in 782. After a Roman victory, Charlemagne marched his prisoners of war to a river and there gave them the choice: be baptized in the name of the Lord Jesus Christ or be beheaded. One after another, heads rolled. A hundred, a thousand, two thousand. By the bloody end of it, 4,500 of them voted with their lives, tacitly saying that if this Jesus was Charlemagne's "Lord," they wanted nothing to do with him.

All this did not escape the Pope's notice. Pope Leo III crowned Charlemagne Emperor of the Holy Roman Empire. The year, 800. Then, 365 years later, the church canonized him. He is now a saint, enshrined in cathedrals, immortalized in icons, revered by millions.

In 1095, under the leadership of Pope Urban II, the Crusades began. The goal was to rid the Holy Land of the unholy people who occupied it. The empire rallied around the Christian flag, and soon an army of Christian soldiers marched off to war.

Jerusalem fell to the Crusaders on July 15, 1099, leaving over 60,000 men, women, and children strewn in the streets. Raymond of Aguilers, who participated in the massacre, wrote:

> With the fall of Jerusalem and its towers one could see marvelous works. Some of the pagans were mercifully beheaded, others pierced by arrows plunged from towers, and yet others, tortured for a long time, were burned to death in searing flames. Piles of heads, hands and feet lay in the houses and streets, and men and knights were running to and fro over corpses.

Though the purging of Jerusalem was the primary objective, it wasn't the only objective. With the cross of Jesus going on before, these Christian soldiers marched onward to the coastal city of Ashkelon. Over 200,000 pagans were purged from the land, as one of the victors wrote, "in the name of our Lord Jesus Christ."

After a decade of genocide, the cross continued to be wielded against pagan strongholds. At last, Constantinople was captured, then ravaged, then razed. The date, April, 12, 1204.

The union between church and state proved an unholy one. By the end of the Crusades, Christians had destroyed some 20–60 million people. The march went onward and ever westward. One European explorer after another—Columbus, Cortes, Vasco da Gama—claimed the lands they discovered as their own. For their own country, their own Christ, their own coffers.

The images that form the historical footage of that era have been edited in the collective memory of many Christians to form a different narrative. The result? A manipulation of the facts not terribly different from the propaganda film produced by the Capitol.

Here is where the spiritual parallels are all too close, and all too incriminating.

THE SOBERING PROPHECY OF THE STORY

What in the World is Happening in the World?
http://youtu.be/YIf9XTKxmtM
14 minutes, 59 seconds

In the ancient world, cities were fortified by walls. On those walls were watchtowers—high places where lookouts called watchmen stood sentry. They scanned the horizon, day and night, one watch relieving the next, 24/7.

They were the early warning system of the community. If they saw billows of dust during the day churning on the horizon, they would alert the city to brace for a sandstorm. If they saw suspicious movements during the night, somewhere on the distant landscape, they would wake the city with their trumpets. It might be an enemy mounting an attack. Then again, it might be nothing but a vagabond wind and a scurry of shadows, chased by the moon.

Writers today are watchmen on the wall of the community, looking out over the horizon. Our job is to stand and watch, to be awake and alert, ready to sound the trumpet.

This book is about a view of the world in the future. One *possible* future, granted. But for me, at least, it is more than possible.

The three major religions in the world—Judaism, Christianity, and Islam—have their beginnings in one earthly father: Abraham. Each predicts a global upheaval in which the world is thrown into chaos, a climactic time in human history referred to as the "Day of the Lord" or "the End Times" or "the End of Days." Each also predicts the coming of an anointed deliverer who will usher in an unprecedented era of peace and prosperity in which the kingdom of God will come and his will shall be done on earth as it is in heaven.

Which religion is right?

On this point, I believe they all are.

I believe that this convulsive heaving of the earth will come sooner rather than later. We are perhaps already well into the throes of labor, approaching the rasping pain of transition. All we can do is breath and brace ourselves for the next contraction.

We have *always* had wars and rumors of them, it could be argued, but the end has not come. We have always had earthquakes and famines, but the end has not come. We have always had gloomers and doomers wearing sandwich boards of some kind or another that read "The End Is Near." But the end has not come.

It feels as though the same people have been crying wolf for years, decades even. On TV and radio, in books and CDs, they have been calling out to us for so long now, we have tuned them out.

Things seem different now. Does it seem that way to you? Could the wolf be at the door, not howling but rather padding around, sniffing, scratching, waiting?

I am not a dogmatist, but we are told, you and I, to watch for signs and to discern them:

> Now learn this lesson from the fig tree: As soon as its twigs get tender and its leaves come out, you know that summer is near. Even so, when you see all these things, you know that it is near, *right at the door*. (Matthew 24:32-33, emphasis mine)

I am not an extremist, but we are told, you and I, to be prepared:

> [Y]ou know very well that the day of the Lord will come like a thief in the night. While people are saying, "Peace and safety," destruction will come on them suddenly, as labor pains on a pregnant woman, and they will not escape. . . . So then, let us not be like others, who are asleep, but let us be awake and sober. (1 Thessalonians 5:2–3, 6)

I am not an alarmist, but we are told, you and I, that alarming things will happen shortly before Jesus returns:

> Nation will rise against nation, and kingdom against kingdom.
> There will be great earthquakes, famines and pestilences in various places, and fearful events and great signs from heaven. (Luke 21:10 –11)

I am not one who sees conspiracies behind every door, but I believe conspiracies will one day take place behind some of those doors, for Jesus himself warned that "at that time many will turn away from the faith and will betray and hate each other, and many false prophets will appear and deceive many people" (Matthew 24:10–11).

I am not an escapist, but we are encouraged, you and I, to understand that our citizenship is not here on earth but in heaven, "and we eagerly await a Savior from there, the Lord Jesus Christ" (Philippians 3:20).

We of all people should be on the wall, waiting for his return, watching for any sign on the horizon that might give hint of it, hoping that today is the day. And if not today, then soon.

Before Jesus left this earth, he told his disciples what things to look for so they would be able to discern the signs that would precede his return. He wanted them to be ready, and waiting; he wants us to be ready too, waiting as they waited.

We know it will get bad before Jesus returns. He told us *how* bad. But he said it a lot, and we heard it a lot, and, well, let's be honest—we changed channels. Either that, or every time we heard anything close to "wolf," we tuned it out.

O>

Unlike the book of Esther—where God is conspicuous by his absence, illustrating the theme of divine providence, where he is not center stage but working behind the scenes—in *The Hunger Games,* not only is God not behind the scenes, he has left the theater.

Here is why.

The Holy Spirit is the only member of the Godhead who is on earth. The Father is in heaven. The Son is seated at his right hand. Before Jesus left, he told his disciples in the Upper Room (John 13—17) that he would send the Holy Spirit to continue his work on earth. For over 2,000 years the Holy Spirit has been hovering over the deep waters of people's hearts, impregnating them with life. For 2,000 years his goodness has graced the earth by restraining evil and limiting its spread. There will come a day, though, when that restraining force will be withdrawn. Paul tells us:

> Concerning the coming of our Lord Jesus Christ and our being gathered to him, we ask you, brothers and sisters, not to become easily unsettled or alarmed by the teaching allegedly from us—whether by a prophecy or by word of mouth or by letter—asserting that the day of the Lord has already come. Don't let anyone deceive you in any way, for that day will not come until the rebellion occurs and the man of lawlessness is revealed, the man doomed to destruction. He will oppose and will exalt himself over everything that is called God or is worshiped, so that he sets himself up in God's temple, proclaiming himself to be God.
>
> Don't you remember that when I was with you I used to tell you these things? And now you know what is holding him back, so that he may be revealed at the proper time. For the secret power of lawlessness is already at work; but *the one who now holds it back will continue to do so till he is taken out of the way.* (2 Thessalonians 2:1—7, emphasis mine)

Paul's words could very well be rendered, "If you think it's bad now, just wait. You ain't seen nuthin' yet."

We don't know who this "man of lawlessness" is or when he will come, but before he does take the world's stage, the Holy Spirit will take the exit. When he does, he will take all his restraining power with him.

If Panem seemed dark, imagine the darkness that is coming to earth.

The Hunger Games exist in a world where hope, like other resources from the 12 districts, is in short supply. It is there, but like the coal from Katniss's district, you have to work hard to find it. Hope can be found in the Everdeen family, but like their cupboards, it is mostly bare. Yet it seems enough to sustain them. At least for now.

There is hope in the kindness of a neighbor like Peeta, who tosses Katniss a loaf of bread as she sits shivering in the rain. There is hope in the love of a sister like Katniss, who tucks you in bed and sings you to sleep. There is hope in the protection of a friend like Gale, who watches over Katniss's family while she competes in the games. There is hope in the land beyond the fences, hope in the bow Katniss has hidden there, hope in the skill she has in using it. There is hope in the hunt and that by sundown there will be something to put on the table.

The hope goes no further.

The games—hopeless as they end up being for the other tributes—offer hope only to the one who survives. If you are the last one standing, there is a better life for you and your district. But at 23 to 1, the odds are ever against you.

Surely—comes a cry from the image of God within us—*surely* we were made for more than just someone else's entertainment. Or someone else's enrichment.

Admiral Ben Moreell, in his article "Of Bread and Circuses," thought so:

> The evil was not in bread and circuses, per se, but in the willingness of the people to sell their rights as free men for full bellies and the excitement of the games which would serve to distract them from the other human hungers which bread and circuses can never appease.

There is no greater human hunger than the gnawing feeling that there must be more to life than what it takes to sustain it or to stimulate it. Jesus said as much when he announced to a hungry crowd that is wasn't physical food they needed but rather spiritual food:

> I am the bread of life. . . . Whoever eats this bread will live forever. This bread is my flesh, which I will give for the life of the world. . . . Very truly I tell you, unless you eat the flesh of the Son of Man and drink his blood, you have no life in you. (John 6:48, 51, 53).

Later, at the Last Supper, we are told that he took bread, gave thanks, broke it, and gave it to his disciples, saying, "This is my body given for you; do this in remembrance of me" (Luke 22:19).

That, says Jesus, is how we are to remember our past.

And that, says Paul, is how we will safeguard our future. "Whenever you eat this bread and drink this cup, you proclaim the Lord's death until he comes" (1 Corinthians 11:26).

Jesus loved his life away, a person at a time, a day at a time, until the last day when he gave the last of his body, the last of his blood, All he asks is that we remember this. For in remembering who he was, we are reminded of who we are. In remembering what he did, we are reminded of what we are to do. And in remembering how he gave his life, we are reminded of how we are to give ours.

The love of Christ is our hope. Writing to fearful Christians living in the increasingly hostile arena that was Rome, Paul reasons with them:

> Who shall separate us from the love of Christ? Shall trouble or hardship or persecution or famine or nakedness or danger or sword? As it is written:
>
> "For your sake we face death all day long; we are considered as sheep to be slaughtered."
>
> No, in all these things we are more than conquerors through him who loved us. For I am convinced that neither death nor life, neither angels nor demons, neither the present nor the future, nor any powers, neither height nor depth, nor anything else in all creation, will be able to separate us from the love of God that is in Christ Jesus our Lord. (Romans 8:35–39)

Because of Christ's love and how it was broken for us and given for us, the odds are now and forever in our favor.

In him is our hope. And because it is in him, it is a hope stronger than fear, a hope that cannot be contained, neither by death, nor tomb, however securely it is sealed or how strongly it is guarded. Neither by prison, regardless how impenetrable, nor persecution, regardless of how unbearable. Neither a Caiaphas nor a Caesar can stop it.

Hebrews 11 has long been referred to as "God's Hall of Faith." And for good reason. Abraham is enshrined there. So is his wife, Sarah, and their son Isaac. A picture of Jacob hangs there. One of Joseph. Moses. A tapestry of Rahab. A bronze of Gideon. One shrine after another—Samson, David, Samuel, and the prophets:

> [W]ho through faith conquered kingdoms, administered justice, and gained what was promised; who shut the mouths of lions, quenched the fury of the flames, and escaped the edge of the sword; whose weakness was turned to strength; and who became powerful in battle and routed foreign armies. Women received back their dead, raised to life again. (vv. 33–35a)

These men, these women, they are the heroes of the faith.
If you read further down the list, the names fade to anonymity:

> There were others who were tortured, refusing to be released so that they might gain an even better resurrection. Some faced jeers and flogging, and even chains and imprisonment. They were put to death by stoning; they were sawed in two; they were killed by the sword. They went about in sheepskins and goatskins, destitute, persecuted and mistreated—the world was not worthy of them. They wandered in deserts and mountains, living in caves and in holes in the ground. (vv. 35–38)

This was their Hunger Games. And these, their tributes.
Who even knows their names, let alone their stories? All the description we have is a parenthetical one at the first part of verse 38—"The world was not worthy of them."
And they were those referred to in the very next chapter of Hebrews:

> Therefore, since we are surrounded by such a great cloud of witnesses, let us throw off everything that hinders and the sin that so easily entangles. And let us run with perseverance the race marked out for us, fixing our eyes on Jesus, the pioneer and perfecter of faith. For the joy set before him he endured the cross, scorning its shame, and sat down at the right hand of the throne of God. Consider

him who endured such opposition from sinners, so that
you will not grow weary and lose heart. (12:1–3)

The imagery is so vivid we can almost see Eric Liddell in slow motion, running across the finish line in *Chariots of Fire;* almost hear the music by Vangelis, stirring us; almost feel the emotion of those in the stadium, rising to their feet, clapping, cheering.

As we watch them, watching him, it's hard to just sit there. We want to jump to our feet and cheer him on. We are spectators now, not participants, yet we feel our hearts beating faster as he rounds the turn for the finish line. In the straightaway, the adrenaline is coursing through us the way it coursed through him. And as he thrusts his chest to cross the finish line, ours swell. His victory feels shared.

I now want to address the young adults who are reading this, those who are fans of the book and the movie. If it is true that your generation is the generation to be here when Jesus returns, then your name has been drawn from the fishbowl. It is *your* turn in the arena. Yours, and that of your generation.

What weapon will you choose? And how will you use it?

There is a scrawl of graffiti on a wall in Palestine: "Your heart is a weapon the size of a fist. Keep fighting. Keep loving."

Good words. Biblical words. Paul tells us that our battle—*our* "Hunger Games"—is spiritual, not physical; so are the weapons and how we are to wield them.

Now is not a time to be hungover. Now is a time to be sober, clear-eyed, and vigilant on that wall. Not when things get better financially. Not when they get better relationally. *Now.*

According to a 2009 profile in *The New Yorker,* when preparing to direct the first *Terminator* movie, James Cameron did research that revealed something important for all of us who sit in the audience, mesmerized by the adventures of others. He studied the ten most successful movies, analyzing everything in hopes of uncovering the secret to their success. What he discovered was that all ten of those films, diverse as they were, had one thing in common: They all told stories about ordinary people in *extraordinary* circumstances.

Ordinary, everyday people, going about their ordinary, everyday lives, until on one of those ordinary days they fall into, or are forced into, some extraordinary situation where they must act.

Like the Depression, the Dust Bowl, or . . .

The Day of the Lord.

All of us, like Frodo in *The Lord of the Rings,* are reluctant heroes, content to idle our lives away in the Shire, bending an elbow at the bar with the other hobbits, smoking our pipes on the porch, singing our lighthearted songs into the wee hours of the night.

Until one day a ring falls into our hands.

Or the name of our younger sister is drawn out of a fishbowl.

When it happens, it's a game changer.

I believe the times we are entering are extraordinary times. Game-changing times.

I believe the best is yet to come. But I also believe we have to go through a dark and painful birth canal to get there, to get to the light, to see colors for the first time, to see the eyes that love us in ways we can't imagine, even in our best dreams.

So what kind of dream *could* imagine such a love? A different one, I'm sure, than any of us has ever dreamed.

Which makes me wonder . . .

How will we ever get to those eyes, those beautiful, adoring eyes . . . unless we dream a different dream?

A different dream. Not the American dream. Not your parents' dream. Not even *your* dream.

Which raises a question: What *are* the dreams God dreams?

What is his dream for the world? His dream for America? For you, for me?

And how can we ever expect to live that dream, if we don't *know* that dream? Dare to imagine it. Imagine the dream God dreamed . . . when he first dreamed of you. Imagine him holding you in his arms, cradling the beginning of the dream that was once you.

Ordinary you.

The love you see in his eyes will take you places, and *through* places, that knowledge alone can't take you. That courage alone can't, or strength alone, or even faith alone.

Take that ordinary you, who now feels loved beyond your wildest dreams, and take whatever extraordinary circumstances you fall into, or are forced into—put them together and fight your way to the finish. You will make it to those eyes.

His love will take you there.

Don't be afraid.

The best is yet to come.

CONCLUSION

A FEW WORDS FOR THE TRIBUTES WHO WILL FIGHT IN THE COMING HUNGER GAMES

Battle of Kruger Park
http://youtu.be/hk_4ACxUFA8
4 minutes, 49 second

Be alert and of sober mind.
Your enemy the devil prowls around like a roaring lion
looking for someone to devour.

1 Peter 5:8

A few words from the hearts of Katniss and Peeta:
Create community everywhere you go—regardless how small a loaf you have to share.

Look for someone shivering in the rain to share it with.

Hold someone who needs holding, and close enough to where you can feel each other's heart.

Sing to someone whose heart is troubled.

Volunteer to take the place of someone who is vulnerable.

Find a good trainer. Listen well. Work hard. Much will be required of you.

In trying to save who you are, don't sacrifice who you are.

Fight for someone else's survival rather than simply your own.

Hold on to your humanity, no matter how savage the arena.

And now a few words from the heart of Haymitch:

You have an enemy that stalks you, waiting when you are most vulnerable to pounce and devour you.

Be alert but not afraid.

Live with a strong herd around you, and never wander far from it.

Lead with your heart; it will guide you well if you guard it well. Love your life away. Like the loaves Jesus blessed and broke and gave away, your life will be multiplied, not diminished.

When you are in the arena, those who went before you will be in the stands, cheering you on.

Be strong; run well. But know that the battle doesn't go to the strong; or the race, to the swift.

A woman is man's best ally, especially if he's his worst enemy.

The image of God is both male and female.

Toughness and tenderness are not mutually exclusive qualities.

Be still, especially when your world is crumbling around you. Know that he is God, even then.

Hope is stronger than fear, but it is not the only thing stronger. According to 1 John 4:18, love casts out fear. The corollary is also true; fear casts out love. Hope is dangerous only when misplaced.

A good movie is not a story made with moving images but with images that move you.

Images are a way God speaks to a world that has forgotten his voice.

Remember the images that have stirred you, especially the images of Jesus on the cross. Remember the body that was broken for you, the blood that was shed for you. Take and eat. This is how you remember the past. This is how you safeguard the future.

Fearful times are coming. Don't be afraid. Your generation was raised up for such a time as this. *You* were raised up for such a time as this.

Finally, a benediction for you and those like you: May the Lord bless you and keep you. May the Lord make his face to shine upon you. And wherever you go, however dark the place or however painful the passage, may you be ever in his favor. Ever and always in his favor.

Amen.

PSALM 46

For the director of music. Of the Sons of Korah. According to alamoth. A song.

God is our refuge and strength, an ever-present help in trouble.
Therefore we will not fear, though the earth give way
and the mountains fall into the heart of the sea,
though its waters roar and foam and the mountains quake
with their surging.
There is a river whose streams make glad the city of God, the
holy place where the Most High dwells.
God is within her, she will not fall; God will help her at break
of day.
Nations are in uproar, kingdoms fall;
he lifts his voice, the earth melts.
The Lord Almighty is with us; the God of Jacob is our fortress.
Come and see what the Lord has done, the desolations he has
brought on the earth.
He makes wars cease to the ends of the earth.
He breaks the bow and shatters the spear; he burns the shields
with fire.
He says, "Be still, and know that I am God; I will be exalted
among the nations, I will be exalted in the earth."
The Lord Almighty is with us; the God of Jacob is our fortress.

APPENDIX

 ## WHAT THE BIBLE SAYS ABOUT THE COMING HUNGER GAMES, THE COMING OF CHRIST, AND THE GENERATION THAT WILL EXPERIENCE BOTH

What Jesus Says about the Times before His Return

Matthew 24 (NIV; parallel passages in Mark 13 and Luke 21:5–36)

1 Jesus left the temple and was walking away when his disciples came up to him to call his attention to its buildings. **2** "Do you see all these things?" he asked. "Truly I tell you, not one stone here will be left on another; every one will be thrown down."

3 As Jesus was sitting on the Mount of Olives, the disciples came to him privately. "Tell us," they said, "when will this happen, and what will be the sign of your coming and of the end of the age?"

4 Jesus answered: "Watch out that no one deceives you. **5** For many will come in my name, claiming, 'I am the Messiah,' and will deceive many. **6** You will hear of wars and rumors of wars, but see to it that you are not alarmed. Such things must happen, but the end is still to come. **7** Nation will rise against nation, and kingdom against kingdom. There will be famines and earthquakes in various places. **8** All these are the beginning of birth pains.

9 "Then you will be handed over to be persecuted and put to death, and you will be hated by all nations because of me. **10** At that time many will turn away from the faith and will betray and hate each other, **11** and many false prophets will appear and deceive many people. **12** Because of the increase of wickedness, the love of most will grow cold, **13** but the one who stands firm to the end will be saved. **14** And this gospel of the kingdom will be preached in the whole world as a testimony to all nations, and then the end will come.

15 "So when you see standing in the holy place 'the abomination that causes desolation,' spoken of through the prophet Daniel—let the reader understand— **16** then let those who are in Judea flee to the mountains. **17** Let no one on the housetop go down to take anything out of the house. **18** Let no one in the field go back to get their cloak. **19** How dreadful it will be in those days for pregnant women and nursing mothers! **20** Pray that your flight will not take place in winter or on the Sabbath. **21** For then there will be great distress, unequaled from the beginning of the world until now—and never to be equaled again.

22 "If those days had not been cut short, no one would survive, but for the sake of the elect those days will be shortened. **23** At that time if anyone says to you, 'Look, here is the Messiah!' or, 'There he is!' do not believe it. **24** For false messiahs and false prophets will appear and perform great signs and wonders to deceive, if possible, even the elect. **25** See, I have told you ahead of time.

26 "So if anyone tells you, 'There he is, out in the wilderness,' do not go out; or, 'Here he is, in the inner rooms,' do not believe it. **27** For as lightning that comes from the east is visible even in the west, so will be the coming of the Son of Man. **28** Wherever there is a carcass, there the vultures will gather.

29 "Immediately after the distress of those days

"'the sun will be darkened, and the moon will not give its light; the stars will fall from the sky, and the heavenly bodies will be shaken.'

30 "Then will appear the sign of the Son of Man in heaven. And then all the peoples of the earth will mourn when they see the Son of Man coming on the clouds of heaven, with power and great glory. **31** And he will send his angels with a loud trumpet call, and they will gather his elect from the four winds, from one end of the heavens to the other.

32 "Now learn this lesson from the fig tree: As soon as its twigs get tender and its leaves come out, you know that summer is near. **33** Even so, when you see all these things, you know that it is near, right at the door.

34 Truly I tell you, this generation will certainly not pass away until all these things have happened. **35** Heaven and earth will pass away, but my words will never pass away.

36 "But about that day or hour no one knows, not even the angels in heaven, nor the Son, but only the Father. **37** As it was in the days of Noah, so it will be at the coming of the Son of Man. **38** For in the days before the flood, people were eating and drinking, marrying and giving in marriage, up to the day Noah entered the ark; **39** and they knew nothing about what would happen until the flood came and took them all away. That is how it will be at the coming of the Son of Man. **40** Two men will be in the field; one will be taken and the other left. **41** Two women will be grinding with a hand mill; one will be taken and the other left.

42 "Therefore keep watch, because you do not know on what day your Lord will come. **43** But understand this: If the owner of the house had known at what time of night the thief was coming, he would have kept watch and would not have let his house be broken into. **44** So you also must be ready, because the Son of Man will come at an hour when you do not expect him.

45 "Who then is the faithful and wise servant, whom the master has put in charge of the servants in his household to give them their food at the proper time? **46** It will be good for that servant whose master finds him doing so when he returns. **47** Truly I tell you, he will put him in charge of all his possessions. **48** But suppose that servant is wicked and says to himself, 'My master is staying away a long time,' **49** and he then begins to beat his fellow servants and to eat and drink with drunkards. **50** The master of that servant will come on a day when he does not expect him and at an hour he is not aware of. **51** He will cut him to pieces and assign him a place with the hypocrites, where there will be weeping and gnashing of teeth."

What Peter Says about Those Times

1 Peter 4:7–8

7 The end of all things is near. Therefore be alert and of sober mind so that you may pray. **8** Above all, love each other deeply, because love covers over a multitude of sins.

2 Peter 3:3–14

3 Above all, you must understand that in the last days scoffers will come, scoffing and following their own evil desires. **4** They will say, "Where is this 'coming' he promised? Ever since our ancestors died, everything goes on as it has since the beginning of creation." **5** But they deliberately forget that long ago by God's word the heavens came into being and the earth was formed out of water and by water. **6** By these waters also the world of that time was deluged and destroyed. **7** By the same word the present heavens and earth are reserved for fire, being kept for the day of judgment and destruction of the ungodly.

8 But do not forget this one thing, dear friends: With the Lord a day is like a thousand years, and a thousand years are like a day. **9** The Lord is not slow in keeping his promise, as some understand slowness. Instead he is patient with you, not wanting anyone to perish, but everyone to come to repentance.

10 But the day of the Lord will come like a thief. The heavens will disappear with a roar; the elements will be destroyed by fire, and the earth and everything done in it will be laid bare.

11 Since everything will be destroyed in this way, what kind of people ought you to be? You ought to live holy and godly lives **12** as you look forward to the day of God and speed its coming. That day will bring about the destruction of the heavens by fire, and the elements will melt in the heat. **13** But in keeping with his promise we are looking forward to a new heaven and a new earth, where righteousness dwells.

14 So then, dear friends, since you are looking forward to this, make every effort to be found spotless, blameless and at peace with him.

What Paul Says about Those Times

1 Timothy 4:1

The Spirit clearly says that in later times some will abandon the faith and follow deceiving spirits and things taught by demons.

2 Timothy 3:1–7

1 But mark this: There will be terrible times in the last days. **2** People will be lovers of themselves, lovers of money, boastful, proud, abusive, disobedient to their parents, ungrateful, unholy, **3** without love, unforgiving, slanderous, without self-control, brutal, not lovers of the good, **4** treacherous, rash, conceited, lovers of pleasure rather than lovers of God—**5** having a form of godliness but denying its power. Have nothing to do with such people.

6 They are the kind who worm their way into homes and gain control over gullible women, who are loaded down with sins and are swayed by all kinds of evil desires, **7** always learning but never able to come to a knowledge of the truth.

1 Thessalonians 5:1–11

1 Now, brothers and sisters, about times and dates we do not need to write to you, **2** for you know very well that the day of the Lord will come like a thief in the night. **3** While people are saying, "Peace and safety," destruction will come on them suddenly, as labor pains on a pregnant woman, and they will not escape.

4 But you, brothers and sisters, are not in darkness so that this day should surprise you like a thief. **5** You are all children of the light and children of the day. We do not belong to the night or to the darkness. **6** So then, let us not be like others, who are asleep, but let us be awake and sober. **7** For those who sleep, sleep at night, and those who get drunk, get drunk at night. **8** But since we belong to the day, let us be sober, putting on faith and love as a breastplate, and the hope of salvation as a helmet. **9** For God did not appoint us to suffer wrath but to receive salvation through our Lord Jesus Christ. **10** He died for us so that, whether we are awake or asleep, we may live together with him. **11** Therefore encourage one another and build each other up, just as in fact you are doing.

2 Thessalonians 2:1–12

1 Concerning the coming of our Lord Jesus Christ and our being gathered to him, we ask you, brothers and sisters, **2** not to become easily unsettled or alarmed by the teaching allegedly from us—whether by a prophecy or by word of mouth or by letter —asserting that the day of the Lord has already come. **3** Don't let anyone deceive you in any way, for that day will not come until the rebellion occurs and the man of lawlessness is revealed, the man doomed to destruction. **4** He will oppose and will exalt himself over everything that is called God or is worshiped, so that he sets himself up in God's temple, proclaiming himself to be God.

5 Don't you remember that when I was with you I used to tell you these things? **6** And now you know what is holding him back, so that he may be revealed at the proper time. **7** For the secret power of lawlessness is already at work; but the one who now holds it back will continue to do so till he is taken out of the way. **8** And then the lawless one will be revealed, whom the Lord Jesus will overthrow with the breath of his mouth and destroy by the splendor of his coming. **9** The coming of the lawless one will be in accordance with how Satan works. He will use all sorts of displays of power through signs and wonders that serve the lie, **10** and all the ways that wickedness deceives those who are perishing. They perish because they refused to love the truth and so be saved. **11** For this reason God sends them a powerful delusion so that they will believe the lie **12** and so that all will be condemned who have not believed the truth but have delighted in wickedness.

The Enemy's Strategy against Us

1 Peter 5:8

Be alert and of sober mind. Your enemy the devil prowls around like a roaring lion looking for someone to devour.

2 Thessalonians 2:8–12

8 And then the lawless one will be revealed, whom the Lord Jesus will overthrow with the breath of his mouth and destroy by the splendor of his coming. **9** The coming of the lawless one will be in accordance with how Satan works. He will use all sorts of displays of power through signs and wonders that serve the lie, **10** and all the ways that wickedness deceives those who are perishing. They perish because they refused to love the truth and so be saved. **11** For this reason God sends them a powerful delusion so that they will believe the lie **12** and so that all will be condemned who have not believed the truth but have delighted in wickedness.

Our Strategy against the Enemy

Ephesians 6:10–18

10 Finally, be strong in the Lord and in his mighty power. **11** Put on the full armor of God, so that you can take your stand against the devil's schemes. **12** For our struggle is not against flesh and blood, but against the rulers, against the authorities, against the powers of this dark world and against the spiritual forces of evil in the heavenly realms. **13** Therefore put on the full armor of God, so that when the day of evil comes, you may be able to stand your ground, and after you have done everything, to stand. **14** Stand firm then, with the belt of truth buckled around your waist, with the breastplate of righteousness in place, **15** and with your feet fitted with the readiness that comes from the gospel of peace. **16** In addition to all this, take up the shield of faith, with which you can extinguish all the flaming arrows of the evil one. **17** Take the helmet of salvation and the sword of the Spirit, which is the word of God.

18 And pray in the Spirit on all occasions with all kinds of prayers and requests. With this in mind, be alert and always keep on praying for all the Lord's people.

James 4:7

Submit yourselves, then, to God. Resist the devil, and he will flee from you.

The Ally Who Fights for Us

John 17:15

My prayer is not that you take them out of the world but that you protect them from the evil one.

Romans 8:34

Who then is the one who condemns? No one. Christ Jesus who died—more than that, who was raised to life—is at the right hand of God and is also interceding for us.

Hebrews 7:25

Therefore he is able to save completely those who come to God through him, because he always lives to intercede for them.

2 Thessalonians 3:3

But the Lord is faithful, and he will strengthen you and protect you from the evil one.

Romans 8:35–39

35 Who shall separate us from the love of Christ? Shall trouble or hardship or persecution or famine or nakedness or danger or sword? **36** As it is written:

"For your sake we face death all day long; we are considered as sheep to be slaughtered."

37 No, in all these things we are more than conquerors through him who loved us. **38** For I am convinced that neither death nor life, neither angels nor demons, neither the present nor the future, nor any powers, **39** neither height nor depth, nor anything else in all creation, will be able to separate us from the love of God that is in Christ Jesus our Lord.

The Ally Who Returns for Us

John 14:1–3

1 Do not let your hearts be troubled. You believe in God; believe also in me. **2** My Father's house has many rooms; if that were not so, would I have told you that I am going there to prepare a place for you? **3** And if I go and prepare a place for you, I will come back and take you to be with me that you also may be where I am.

Acts 1:9–11

9 After he said this, he was taken up before their very eyes, and a cloud hid him from their sight.

10 They were looking intently up into the sky as he was going, when suddenly two men dressed in white stood beside them. **11** "Men of Galilee," they said, "why do you stand here looking into the sky? This same Jesus, who has been taken from you into heaven, will come back in the same way you have seen him go into heaven."

Revelation 22:10–21

10 Then he told me, "Do not seal up the words of the prophecy of this scroll, because the time is near. **11** Let the one who does wrong continue to do wrong; let the vile person continue to be vile; let the one who does right continue to do right; and let the holy person continue to be holy."

12 "Look, I am coming soon! My reward is with me, and I will give to each person according to what they have done. **13** I am the Alpha and the Omega, the First and the Last, the Beginning and the End.

14 "Blessed are those who wash their robes, that they may have the right to the tree of life and may go through the gates into the city. **15** Outside are the dogs, those who practice magic arts, the sexually immoral, the murderers, the idolaters and everyone who loves and practices falsehood.

16 "I, Jesus, have sent my angel to give you this testimony for the churches. I am the Root and the Offspring of David, and the bright Morning Star."

17 The Spirit and the bride say, "Come!" And let the one who hears say, "Come!" Let the one who is thirsty come; and let the one who wishes take the free gift of the water of life.

18 I warn everyone who hears the words of the prophecy of this scroll: If anyone adds anything to them, God will add to that person the plagues described in this scroll. **19** And if anyone takes words away from this scroll of prophecy, God will take away from that person any share in the tree of life and in the Holy City, which are described in this scroll.

20 He who testifies to these things says, "Yes, I am coming soon." Amen. Come, Lord Jesus.

21 The grace of the Lord Jesus be with God's people. Amen.

The Hope that Sustains Us during Difficult Times

Lamentations 3:19–23

19 I remember my affliction and my wandering, the bitterness and the gall. **20** I well remember them, and my soul is downcast within me. **21** Yet this I call to mind and therefore I have hope:

22 Because of the LORD's great love we are not consumed, for his compassions never fail. **23** They are new every morning; great is your faithfulness.

Romans 5:1–5

1 Therefore, since we have been justified through faith, we have peace with God through our Lord Jesus Christ, **2** through whom we have gained access by faith into this grace in which we now stand. And we boast in the hope of the glory of God. **3** Not only so, but we also glory in our sufferings, because we know that suffering produces perseverance; **4** perseverance, character; and character, hope. **5** And hope does not put us to shame, because God's love has been poured out into our hearts through the Holy Spirit, who has been given to us.

Romans 8:18–29

18 I consider that our present sufferings are not worth comparing with the glory that will be revealed in us. **19** For the creation waits in eager expectation for the children of God to be revealed. **20** For the creation was subjected to frustration, not by its own choice, but by the will of the one who subjected it, in hope **21** that the creation itself will be liberated from its bondage to decay and brought into the freedom and glory of the children of God.

22 We know that the whole creation has been groaning as in the pains of childbirth right up to the present time. **23** Not only so, but we ourselves, who have the firstfruits of the Spirit, groan inwardly as we wait eagerly for our adoption to sonship, the redemption of our bodies. **24** For in this hope we were saved. But hope that is seen is no hope at all. Who hopes for what they already have? **25** But if we hope for what we do not yet have, we wait for it patiently.

26 In the same way, the Spirit helps us in our weakness. We do not know what we ought to pray for, but the Spirit himself intercedes for us through wordless groans. **27** And he who searches our hearts knows the mind of the Spirit, because the Spirit intercedes for God's people in accordance with the will of God.

28 And we know that in all things God works for the good of those who love him, who have been called according to his purpose. **29** For those God foreknew he also predestined to be conformed to the image of his Son, that he might be the firstborn among many brothers and sisters.

Romans 15:13

May the God of hope fill you with all joy and peace as you trust in him, so that you may overflow with hope by the power of the Holy Spirit.

The Memory that Safeguards Us during Difficult Times

John 6:48–56

48 "I am the bread of life. **49** Your ancestors ate the manna in the wilderness, yet they died. **50** But here is the bread that comes down from heaven, which anyone may eat and not die. **51** I am the living bread that came down from heaven. Whoever eats this bread will live forever. This bread is my flesh, which I will give for the life of the world."

52 Then the Jews began to argue sharply among themselves, "How can this man give us his flesh to eat?"

53 Jesus said to them, "Very truly I tell you, unless you eat the flesh of the Son of Man and drink his blood, you have no life in you. **54** Whoever eats my flesh and drinks my blood has eternal life, and I will raise them up at the last day. **55** For my flesh is real food and my blood is real drink. **56** Whoever eats my flesh and drinks my blood remains in me, and I in them."

Luke 22:14–20

14 When the hour came, Jesus and his apostles reclined at the table. **15** And he said to them, "I have eagerly desired to eat this Passover with you before I suffer. **16** For I tell you, I will not eat it again until it finds fulfillment in the kingdom of God."

17 After taking the cup, he gave thanks and said, "Take this and divide it among you. **18** For I tell you I will not drink again from the fruit of the vine until the kingdom of God comes."

19 And he took bread, gave thanks and broke it, and gave it to them, saying, "This is my body given for you; do this in remembrance of me."

20 In the same way, after the supper he took the cup, saying, "This cup is the new covenant in my blood, which is poured out for you."

1 Corinthians 11:23–26

23 For I received from the Lord what I also passed on to you: The Lord Jesus, on the night he was betrayed, took bread, **24** and when he had given thanks, he broke it and said, "This is my body, which is for you; do this in remembrance of me." **25** In the same way, after supper he took the cup, saying, "This cup is the new covenant in my blood; do this, whenever you drink it, in remembrance of me." **26** For whenever you eat this bread and drink this cup, you proclaim the Lord's death until he comes.

The Words that Encourage Us during Difficult Times

Be calm—Philippians 4:6–8

6 Do not be anxious about anything, but in every situation, by prayer and petition, with thanksgiving, present your requests to God. **7** And the peace of God, which transcends all understanding, will guard your hearts and your minds in Christ Jesus.

8 Finally, brothers and sisters, whatever is true, whatever is noble, whatever is right, whatever is pure, whatever is lovely, whatever is admirable—if anything is excellent or praiseworthy—think about such things.

Be alert—1 Peter 5:8

Be alert and of sober mind. Your enemy the devil prowls around like a roaring lion looking for someone to devour.

Be ready—Matthew 24:44

So you also must be ready, because the Son of Man will come at an hour when you do not expect him.

Be strong—Ephesians 6:10

Finally, be strong in the Lord and in his mighty power.

Be patient—James 5:7–11

7 Be patient, then, brothers and sisters, until the Lord's coming. See how the farmer waits for the land to yield its valuable crop, patiently waiting for the autumn and spring rains. **8** You too, be patient and stand firm, because the Lord's coming is near. **9** Don't grumble against one another, brothers and sisters, or you will be judged. The Judge is standing at the door!

10 Brothers and sisters, as an example of patience in the face of suffering, take the prophets who spoke in the name of the Lord. **11** As you know, we count as blessed those who have persevered. You have heard of Job's perseverance and have seen what the Lord finally brought about. The Lord is full of compassion and mercy.

Be joyful—James 1:2–4

2 Consider it pure joy, my brothers and sisters, whenever you face trials of many kinds, **3** because you know that the testing of your faith produces perseverance. **4** Let perseverance finish its work so that you may be mature and complete, not lacking anything.

Be faithful—Matthew 25:21

His master replied, "Well done, good and faithful servant! You have been faithful with a few things; I will put you in charge of many things. Come and share your master's happiness!"

Be a person who loves your life away—1 Peter 4:7–11

7 The end of all things is near. Therefore be alert and of sober mind so that you may pray. **8** Above all, love each other deeply, because love covers over a multitude of sins. **9** Offer hospitality to one another without grumbling. **10** Each of you should use whatever gift you have received to serve others, as faithful stewards of God's grace in its various forms. **11** If anyone speaks, they should do so as one who speaks the very words of God. If anyone serves, they should do so with the strength God provides, so that in all things God may be praised through Jesus Christ. To him be the glory and the power for ever and ever. Amen.

Be blameless—2 Peter 3:10–14

10 But the day of the Lord will come like a thief. The heavens will disappear with a roar; the elements will be destroyed by fire, and the earth and everything done in it will be laid bare.

11 Since everything will be destroyed in this way, what kind of people ought you to be? You ought to live holy and godly lives **12** as you look forward to the day of God and speed its coming. That day will bring about the destruction of the heavens by fire, and the elements will melt in the heat. **13** But in keeping with his promise we are looking forward to a new heaven and a new earth, where righteousness dwells.

14 So then, dear friends, since you are looking forward to this, make every effort to be found spotless, blameless and at peace with him.

ENDNOTES

Frontispiece quote

From *The Hunger Games* by Suzanne Collins (New York: Scholastic Press, Inc., 2008), back cover.

Part I The Cinematic Story

The quote is from *The World of the Hunger Games* by Kate Egan (New York: Scholastic Press, Inc., 2012), 5.

Chapter 2 The Seminal Precursors to the Story

The quote about saving the cat is from *Save the Cat!* by Blake Snyder (Studio City, CA: Michael Wiese Productions, 2005), xv.

For those interested in the differences between the film and the book from which it was adapted, see the Wikipedia article on The Hunger Games (http://thehungergames.wikia.com/wiki/The_Hunger_Games_book_to_film_differences).

The dialogue quotes are from the film. Lionsgate Entertainment, 2012. The screenwriters were Gary Ross, Suzanne Collins, and Billy Ray.

Chapter 3 The Strong Protagonist in the Story

The quote about female action heroes is from "Film Females Join the Fight Club," an article by Susan Wloszczyna in *USA Today*, July 27, 2012, 1B.

The quote about Katniss being a hunter is from "Jennifer Lawrence on *The Hunger Games*: It's not *Twilight*," by Krista Smith. VF Daily/Vanity Fair. com. (November 2, 2011, http://www.vanityfair.com/online/daily/2011/11/jennifer-lawrence-the-hunger-games-twilight).

Research for the Hebrew word for "helper" came from the *Theological Wordbook of the Old Testament,* R. Laird Harris, Gleason L. Archer, Jr., Bruce K. Waltke. Volume 2 (Chicago: Moody Press, 1980), entry #1598.

Research for the Hebrew word for "valor" came from the *Theological Wordbook of the Old Testament,* entry #624.

The quote about "a female warrior worth cheering," is from the movie review, "The Hunger Games," by Peter Travers. Rolling Stone Reviews/RollingStone.com. (March 21, 2012, http://www.rollingstone.com/movies/reviews/the-hunger-games-20120321).

The quote about fighting like a girl is by Susan Wloszczyna, *USA Today,* "Film Females Join the Fight Club" (July 27, 2012), 1B.

Part II The Contemporary Story

"The Inevitable Decline of Decadence" by Adrienne Kress in *The Girl Who Was on Fire,* edited by Leah Wilson (Dallas: BenBella Books, 2011), 230.

Chapter 4 The Social Phenomenon of the Story

The quote on character and image is from *When No One Sees: The Importance of Character in an Age of Image* by Os Guiness (Colorado Springs: NavPress, 2000), 187.

The quote about how fast the world has changed is from *That Used to Be Us* by Thomas L. Friedman and Michael Mendelbaum (New York: Strauss & Giroux, 2001), 59.

Chapter 5 The Societal Pictures in the Story

The quote about Bobby Martin is from the short story in *The New Yorker,* "The Lottery" by Shirley Jackson, June 26, 1948, 25-28. The short story can be read in its entirety by going to the archives of the magazine (http://archives.newyorker.com/?i=1948-06-26#folio=CVI), or check your local library.

The quote by Juvenal is from *Satires,* Juvenal, "Satire X: The Vanity of Human Wishes," 10.81.

The story of Telemachus is from Book V, Chapter XXVI, "Of Honorius the Emperor and Telemachus the monk" in *The Ecclesiastical History of Theodoret,* (Whitefish, MT: Kessinger Publishing LLC : 2010), 196.

The quotation about the Reaping is from the essay "Someone to Watch Over Me" by Lili Wilkinson in *The Girl Who Was on Fire,* edited by Leah Wilson (Dallas, TX: BenBella Books, Inc., 2010), 72.

Part III The Coming Story

Chapter 6 The Spiritual Parallels in the Story

The quotation on ignorance is by Will Rogers and was cited in *The New York Times,* August 31, 1924.

Research on the Crusades was done in the following books:

The History of the Crusades by Joseph Francois Michaud. Volume I (New York: A. C. Armstrong & Son, 1895).

Sacred Violence: The European Crusades to the Middle East, 1095–1396 by Jill N. Claster (Toronto: University of Toronto Press, 2009).

Crusade Propaganda and Ideology by Christopher T. Maier (Cambridge: Cambridge University Press, 2000).

The First Crusaders, 1095–1131 (especially chapter 3, "Preaching and the Crusades") by Jonathan Riley-Smith (Cambridge: Cambridge University Press, 1997), 53–80.

Jerusalem in the Time of the Crusades by Adrian J. Boas (New York: Routledge, 2001).

The quote by Raymond of Aguilers is from *Competing Voices from the Crusades* by Andrew Holt and James Muldoon (Westport, Connecticut: Greenwood World Publishing, 2008), 49.

Chapter 7 The Sobering Prophecy of the Story

The quote about the heart being a weapon is from the essay "Your Heart is a Weapon the Size of Your Fist" by Mary Borsellino in *The Girl Who Was on Fire,* edited by Leah Wilson (Dallas: BenBella Books, Inc., 2011), 30.

The quote about bread and circuses is from "Of Bread and Circuses" by Admiral Ben Moreell, *The Freeman.* Volume 6, issue 1, January, 1956.